MILLION
DOLLAR HOST

Julie's Airbnb Portfolio
Earned Over A Million Dollars In
Her First Year... Yours Can Too!

JULIE GEORGE

In Praise of Julie George

From Airbnb property owners –

"We were looking for an investment property when Julie introduced us to the world of Airbnb. She guided us to an inner-city unit that was in our budget and desired location. We engaged the Airbnb management services Julie offered and were very impressed with the rental return. As well as the financial gains, we also liked that we could use the property ourselves when we want and the property is well maintained and cleaned regularly. We have been so happy with the Airbnb management of our property we have recently purchased a second unit and repeated the process with Julie and her team. We highly recommend property investors seek Julie's expert advice when it comes to Airbnb."

—Gary & Sue Struber, Cairns QLD

From Airbnb entrepreneurs building their own successful businesses –

"Julie George from Host My Home has been an instrumental part in the setting up our successful Airbnb management business. Julie is incredibly easy to communicate with and is constantly exceeding our expectations by providing us with prompt, reliable and knowledgeable advice. Julie enabled us to structure our Airbnb business the right way from the beginning which has saved us a lot of time and money. Even now, after one year of operations, we still find our conversations with Julie incredibly helpful."

—Mel and Nadja, Team BnB, Noosa QLD

"It was a daunting task for me to venture out and start my own business until I came across the services of Julie George from Host My Home. Julie mentored me through the process of establishing and growing 'BNB Made Easy' making sure all bases were covered. The level of experience and expertise Julie provides is absolutely priceless. Her astonishing success speaks for itself and I highly recommend Julie's professional services to anyone wanting to create or develop a <u>successful</u> short-term rental business."

—Tim Mortimer, BNB Made Easy, Orange NSW

"When setting up my business in Airbnb management, I came across a few hurdles and reached out to Julie George from Host My Home. It was Easter Sunday and not expecting to get a response until the following week Julie responded within the hour, very impressive keeping up her response rate even with her consulting clients. Julie called me that afternoon as she said she would. Seriously, who does that, it was Easter Sunday!!! Julie's guidance and expertise to all my requests has certainly saved me a lot of time, money and hair pulling. Julie is real and super lovely and knowing I can contact her at anytime is priceless. I cannot recommend Julie highly enough if you are seeking successful advice in the Airbnb world!"

—Tanya Tempest, Soulfull Stayz, Sunshine Coast QLD

Julie George and Host My Home Pty Ltd have no affiliation with Airbnb other than being a VERY happy and satisfied customer, who highly recommends this platform above all others in the marketplace.

© 2018 Julie George All rights reserved.
© 2018 Million Dollar Host All rights reserved.
Website: www.milliondollarhost.com.au
Email: julie@milliondollarhost.com.au

No part of this publication may be reproduced, distributed, or transmitted in any form or by any means, including photocopying, recording, or other electronic or mechanical methods, without the prior written permission of the publisher, except in the case of brief quotations embodied in critical reviews and certain other non-commercial uses permitted by copyright law.

Limit of Liability/Disclaimer of Warranty.

While the publisher and author have used their best efforts in preparing this book, they make no representations or warranties with respect to the accuracy or completeness of the contents of this book and specifically disclaim any implied warranties or merchantability or fitness for a particular purpose. No warranty may be created or extended by sales representatives or written sales material. The advice and strategies contained herein is intended for a general audience and does not purport to be, nor should it be construed as, specific advice tailored to any individual and may not be suitable for your situation.

There is no guarantee, express or implied, that you will earn any money using the techniques and ideas in this book. Examples in these materials are not to be interpreted as a promise or guarantee of earnings. Earning potential is entirely dependent on the efforts and skills of the person applying all or part of the concepts, ideas and strategies contained herein.

Neither the publisher not the author shall be liable for any loss of profit or any other commercial damages, including but not limited to special, incidental, consequential, or other damages.

Best Seller Success Publishing
Las Vegas, Nevada, USA
+1 (702) 997 2229
Sydney, Australia
+61 (02) 8005 4868

Dedication

I would like to thank my husband.... Mark has always joked that this is how I should start all my speeches or book dedications. Finally, I have an opportunity to do so and I am eternally grateful for the support and patience he has shown during the book writing process and the hours I have dedicated to the world of Airbnb. I would also like to thank my team at Host My Home, my family, friends and Cydney OSullivan (who was instrumental in this book seeing the light of day).

Table of Contents

FOREWORD 1
ABOUT THE AUTHOR 3
INTRODUCTION 5
STATS AND NUMBERS 9
MY STORY 13
    Inverell to Los Angeles 13
    Sydney to Alice Springs 18
    Cairns and An Introduction to Property 21
    Small Business and the Corporate World 28
    Airbnb Turned My Life Upside Down 34

AIRBNB BASICS 51
    What is Airbnb? 51
    How Can Airbnb Change Your Life? 53
    Rent a Room in Your House 55
    Rent Out Your Home While You Are on Holidays 57
    Rent Out Your Investment Property 59
    Buy Yourself a Holiday Home 61

LET'S GET STARTED... CREATING A LISTING & MAKING THE MOST OF IT! 65
    Essentials for Setting Up an Airbnb Property 65
    Consumables and Gifts for Guests 70

    Steps to a Successful Listing 72
    Reviews/Follow-Up with Guests 88
    Guests Caused Damage — Now What? 89

BUILDING A BUSINESS USING THE AIRBNB SYSTEM 93
    Establish an Airbnb Property Management Company 94
    Become a Co-Host 101
    Leasing/Sub-Leasing 103
    List an Experience on Airbnb 105
    List Your Restaurant/Café/Eatery on Airbnb 106
    Provide Third-Party Services to Hosts 106
    Create a Booking Agency for Airbnb Listings 107
    Offer a Consulting Service 109
    Earn Travel Credit 110
    Work as a Buyer's Agent with Investors 111

WHERE TO FIND NEW LISTINGS 113
    Traditional Marketing Options 113
    Online Marketing Options 114
    Contacting Existing Hosts 115
    Networking Opportunities 115
    Professional Referrals 117
    Finder's Fee 118

MY SECRETS TO SUCCESS 119
    Surround Yourself with a Great Team 119
    Take a Risk — What's the Worst That Could Happen? 120
    Dream Big and Scale 121

Foreword

The stars were aligned when Julie George took her first foray into Airbnb. With a background in both tourism and real estate, it makes sense that she would link the two and create a new business model for property management across the gargantuan lettings site.

From feeding Salties in the Northern Territory to promoting Australia to American tourists hungry for a taste of Crocodile Dundee's outback, Julie has remained loyal to her roots by encouraging tourism in her homeland.

Julie is recognised as one of Australia's leading experts on Airbnb and is the owner/manager of one of Australia's leading Airbnb Property Management companies located in Far North Queensland.

Julie's generous nature extends to sharing her hard work and knowledge in Million Dollar Host, making it possible for anyone, anywhere to set up a similar business. There's no reason why you, sitting in London, Moscow, Timbuktu or a tiny island off mainland China can't do the same, and what's more, Julie positively encourages you to do so.

In no time at all, you, like Julie, can enjoy financial freedom and the pleasure of, amongst other things, your own bar fridge. Consider Million Dollar Host as a gift from the world's most generous hostess.

Cheers to that and all that Million Dollar Host brings.

—**Pat Mesiti,** international motivational speaker, the author of *Pathway to Prosperity: The 12 Steps to Financial Freedom*, *Staying Together Without Falling Apart: How to Thrive in a Modern-Day Relationship* and other best-selling books.

About The Author

Julie George is the owner of Host My Home Pty Ltd, a unique Airbnb property management company in Cairns, Queensland that offers a full management service along with consultation options for property owners wanting help to get into the Airbnb market.

She is recognized as one of the Australia's top Airbnb hosts with her portfolio of properties bringing in millions of dollars each year. Julie has been featured in the Cairns Life Magazine, Cairns Post, Channel 7 and Win TV as a leading Airbnb expert in Australia.

Julie is also a registered real estate agent with experience in marketing and hospitality who has also mentored others wanting to establish their own Airbnb property management business. Motivating budding entrepreneurs and mentoring others to build a similar business to her own is one of Julie's passions.

Julie George is available as a Professional Speaker and welcomes the opportunity to address 'like minded' entrepreneurs looking for an opportunity to build a business of their own on the back of the sharing economy. If you would like Julie to speak at your next event you can contact her at julie@milliondollarhost.com.au

Introduction

I have always been one for setting a goal and then making it happen! Some of my more recent goals, set in 2016, were:

1. To establish a business that was innovative and different from what others were already doing in the marketplace. I also wanted to have a business that I could scale up and could be adopted anywhere in the world.

> I have always been one for setting a goal and then making it happen!

2. To create financial freedom so that I didn't have to work for someone else to pay my bills.

3. To work *on* my new business, not *in* it, so that I could continue to develop new ideas and have an awesome life where I could travel and not be trapped behind a desk 12 hours a day.

4. To develop a business idea that not only changed my life for the better but also those of others (e.g., employees and other like-minded entrepreneurs).

5. To not have to borrow any money to create this business for myself — I didn't want to get into debt for the sake of a new business idea.

6. To find a business idea where I didn't have to chase money. I wanted reassurance that my payments would be collected for me.

7. To have my own office, parking, and a mini-fridge under my desk.

Less than 18 months after setting this goal, I now find myself writing about it — because I have achieved all the above!

I am the director of Host My Home Pty Ltd Airbnb Property Management, one of the fastest-growing new business concepts in Australia, riding the success of the sharing economy. The business offers property investors an alternative to traditional real estate options, generally making them a lot more money than long-term rentals, and giving them the freedom and flexibility to use their own properties. This business is built on a structure that is easily scaled up and adapted anywhere in the world.

In my first year of business, my Airbnb portfolio brought in $1.4 million in bookings and in my second year, that number is forecast to double. The team I have working with me have been trained to operate the business without my personal input allowing me the flexibility for family time, travel and special projects such as writing this book.

I employ a team of locals who have also had their lives changed by this new business concept. I have helped other like-minded entrepreneurs establish their own property management businesses, along with individuals who wanted to create their own Airbnb listing to self-manage. I didn't have to borrow any money to launch my business and in total, I put in just over $9,000 during my first year of business.

Airbnb has provided the most amazing platform for my business — they do all the marketing I need to enable millions of travelers around the world to view my properties, they collect the payments for me so there is no worries or anxieties associated with the finances, and on top of that, they offer an impressive support system should things go wrong.

My new goal is to share my knowledge and experience with others. In this book, you will find out more about me, my background and how I now find myself in this fortunate position of being able to coach others to financial freedom. I have discovered multiple ways of earning a great income on Airbnb without necessarily having to own any property, and hope that one of these ideas may just be the one to change your life for the better!

Stats And Numbers

The first question I always have when someone is promoting a business success is …'Show Me?' I want proof that the "so called Expert" in the field has done the hard work and actually succeeded in their business endeavors before I spend a cent to buy their product or in this case…book. I am just hoping that as you are flicking through the book while you stand in the book shop that perhaps you have landed on this page!

As this book goes through the final stages of publishing (in August 2018) we have just experienced our most amazing month ever –

> July 2018 earnings **$390,106.88**

> Airbnb Property Listings – **96**

Below is a graph showing my portfolio income on Airbnb in 2017 and 2018

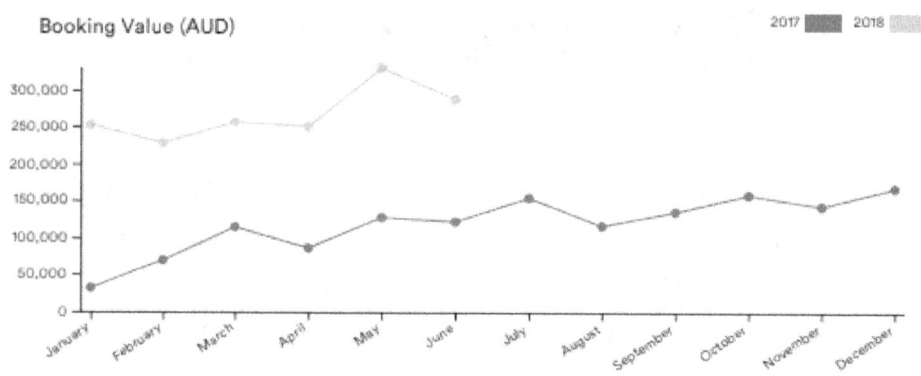

Month	2017	2018	Δ
January	31,400.30	252,415.30	+704%
February	70,136.92	227,873.13	+225%
March	114,182.93	256,187.23	+124%
April	86,711.07	250,890.09	+189%
May	128,475.88	329,326.48	+156%
June	122,738.23	288,470.76	+135%
July	154,592		n/a
August	115,808.05		n/a
September	134,933.08		n/a
October	158,267.03		n/a
November	142,969.55		n/a
December	168,309.98		n/a
Total	1,428,525.02	1,605,162.99	

The graph below shows the increase in my property portfolio in 2017 and 2018

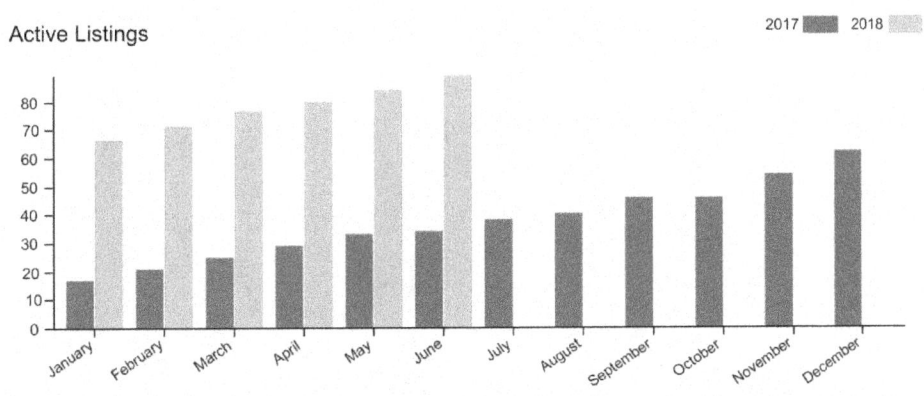

Month	2017	2018	Δ
January	17	66	+288%
February	21	71	+238%
March	25	77	+208%
April	29	80	+176%
May	33	84	+155%
June	34	89	+162%
July	38		n/a
August	40		n/a
September	46		n/a
October	46		n/a
November	54		n/a
December	62		n/a
Average	37.08	77.83	

**1% of Airbnb Hosts have more than 2 listings...
Read on to find out how to join this exclusive club!**

My Story

Inverell to Los Angeles

Everything happens for a reason!

Looking back, all my experiences (good and bad) and the people I have met (again, good and bad) over the years have all inspired the position I find myself in today. Reflecting on my past while writing this book, I realized that some of the mentors or inspiring people I looked up to over the years have shaped my attitude and determination to succeed. Don't get me wrong — some of the people I've met in the past, and their actions, have also inspired me *not* to do the same as them!

Two of the most influential people in my life are of course my parents. My dad, Gordon Scarrow, relocated in the early seventies from New Zealand to Inverell in New South Wales, Australia to be closer to his sister. Having a dairy farming background, he gained employment in the earthmoving industry. It was in Inverell that he met my mother, Suzanne Bell, a local girl who was working as a legal secretary and had not long graduated top of her class from the local high school.

> **Everything happens for a reason!**

They were soon married and in 1975, welcomed me into the world. I must have been a dream baby as they went on to have two more daughters, Jennie and Sally. Inverell was our home for the first five years of my life before Dad was offered an exciting opportunity in the Northern Territory. A family that he'd worked for in the Sapphire Mining Industry in Inverell had decided to have a 'sea change' and open up a tourist park in Kakadu.

Dad was encouraged to join them and be involved in the establishment of the well-known South Alligator Motor Inn (later known as the Kakadu Holiday Village). This move to the top of Australia, miles away from friends and family, was an incredible leap of faith and highly ambitious. In the early eighties, Kakadu was very different to now, notably because you could swim in the waterways back then without fear of a crocodile attack. The croc numbers were low because hunting was still legal.

Most of my schooling took place in Jabiru, a small uranium mining township where everyone knew each other. I formed incredibly strong bonds with school friends at Jabiru and we all grew up exploring the bush, riding go-carts across the floodplains and fishing in the local rivers. I remember our pet water buffalo fondly — the wild pigs that would chase us and scare the living daylights out of us… not so fondly!

The adults in my life at this time were hugely inspiring and building quite the tourism empire across the Territory. The business my family was involved in incorporated resorts and boat cruises from Kings Canyon North to Katherine Gorge, Kakadu, and Darwin. I watched this success and growth unfold in front of me, and I was truly inspired.

By the early nineties, Mum and Dad had separated, leaving Mum a single mother to three young girls. It was at this time that I watched her stand up on her own two feet and go back to full-time study. She was aiming to become a psychologist, which was a long process, but she achieved her goal and is now among the best in her field. She never gave up on her dream and proved to be a positive role model for her daughters.

We relocated to Darwin so I could continue my education past Year 10, which was all my small school in Kakadu catered to. After graduating from high school, I chose to study for a Diploma of Business, majoring in hospitality management. I had been living in resorts and hotels all my life, so it seemed a natural choice.

During this time, I worked in my first job, which was feeding crocodiles on the Jumping Crocodile Cruise at the Adelaide River, just outside Darwin. Dad was the skipper of the boat and I was the hostess. We would fill the boat up with tourists from all over the world and take them on an adventure to see some of the most amazing crocodiles and other wildlife in its natural habitat. Once I spotted a croc, I would tie some pork on the end of a biodegradable string attached to the end of a bamboo stick.

As the meat splashed around in the water, the croc would swim over in the hope of a feed. Crocodiles can jump their full body length out of the water, so with the feeding stick (and good timing!), we could put on quite a show for our visitors. Dad was the ultimate entertainer and became a mini-celebrity, charming thousands of tourists over the years with his tall stories and humor. As luck would have it, just as I completed my studies, Dad and his business partners sold the business to a large conglomerate and my plans to join the company took a different turn — but an exciting one!

In 1995, through an opportunity advertised at Charles Darwin University, I was recruited by a marketing company based in Culver City in Los Angeles, California. I was a trainee sales representative promoting the Northern Territory Tourist Commission in the USA, Canada, and Central and South America. What an opportunity!

One thing I have always done was dream big. One of my goals as a teenager was to go to Hollywood and drive a red convertible… because why not, right?

Flying all over the states, addressing travel agents about the sights and attractions of the Northern Territory was my dream job at the time. The movies *Crocodile Dundee* and *Priscilla Queen of the Desert* were fresh in Americans' minds, so I had to answer a lot of questions to clear up some misunderstandings about Australia.

I got to attend events such as Australian movie premieres where I got to mingle with many Australian movie and TV stars, including Simon Baker Denny, Julian McMahon, Jacqueline McKenzie and another Australian celebrity who offered me cocaine in a bathroom. Which I politely declined, of course… best I keep that particular name to myself!

My mentor at the time was my boss, who was inspirational in growing his own business to one that now has offices in New York and Los Angeles. He had no fear holding him back and set himself goals to achieve what seemed impossible. He didn't just want to promote Australia as a tourism destination to Americans. He also got the contracts to promote many other desirable locations such as South

Africa and the Melanesian Islands. Of course, this meant traveling to these locations to gain the knowledge to market them correctly — what a great businessman! I wonder if a little bit of his ambition and determination might have rubbed off a little on a teenager from the Northern Territory...

A story that ran in the NT News newspaper in 1996

This was such a unique experience and living in the States was a real eye-opener. I made some amazing friends who welcomed me into their family and even took me on holidays to their home country of Nicaragua and Costa Rica. I still remember the challenge of traveling through Nicaragua where no one spoke English (except for the taxi driver singing along to Madonna's *Like a Virgin*). It was a total culture shock but a good one that I have never forgotten. And yes, for those of you wondering… I also managed to achieve my goal of buying and driving a red convertible around Hollywood!

Sydney to Alice Springs

A return to Australia in 1996 saw me landing in Sydney to work with the Northern Territory Tourist Commission. Promoting the Territory as a tourist destination to the people of New South Wales wasn't quite as thrilling as selling it to the Americans, but it did bring me back closer to my friends and family.

> It was inspiring to see how he grew his business and in turn, was able to afford nice things

My uncle took me in when I arrived back in Australia and supported me in getting back on my feet including going guarantor on a car loan. He owned a successful communications and cabling business where he managed a large staff. It was inspiring to see how he grew his business and in turn, was able to afford nice things, including property in the expensive Sydney real estate market. It stuck with me that it is possible to grow your own business and if successful, it can provide very well for you and your family.

Sydney was hustle and bustle of a different kind — it was more hectic than LA, and the daily public transport run on the trains eventually wore me down, less than a year after arriving. It was time to head back to the Territory.

Lucky to have made great contacts through my Sydney posting, I was able to secure a position as marketing manager for one of the popular tour operators in Alice Springs. This company ran aboriginal cultural tours in the morning and bush tucker dinners at night. It was quite the combination and easy to promote to visiting tourists wanting exposure to the Australian way of life.

It was during this time that I met my first husband and shortly after, in September 1998, our son Joshua was born at Alice Springs Hospital. It was an absolute joy to have a son, but to say the birth was a traumatic experience would be an understatement. A horror birth story is not why you're reading this book, so I'll just summarize by saying having a priest at the side of the bed giving me the last rites was not in my birth plan!

Once I was well enough after Joshua's birth, I wanted and needed to find a way to earn some income. My new husband wasn't earning very much in the hospitality industry. It was time to get moving and find some skills I could earn some money with. A neighbor was running a secretarial business that I took over as she was leaving town — and thus, Central Secretarial was born. We offered secretarial services to businesses needing documents typed up and job seekers wanting resumes and cover letters created for them. This was something I could do from home and often had baby Josh in a bouncer under my desk.

The Cartoon Logo trend begins.

Julie and baby Josh in Alice Springs, 1998.

Cairns and An Introduction to Property

Relocating to Cairns in 2000, I found myself starting fresh with a 15-month-old baby, living in a shared house and relying on my husband's income. It was not a comfortable situation for me — I craved my independence and didn't like having to rely on others for financial support. Looking back now, it didn't ever occur to me to go to Centrelink for support. I just had to find a way to make my own income.

> I just had to find a way to make my own income

At that time, there was a culture of chain letters (now I would call it a "scam" rather than a "culture") and I remember putting hours and hours into this project that promised that I would receive money in the mail if I sent a letter off to so many other people. I quickly realized this was a waste of time and stamps, and focused my energies on finding work.

I also was attracted to the lure of party plan sales and got involved with a number of these schemes, with the hope that I would be the one in a million who makes a lot of money out of these home based businesses. I came crashing down to earth each time I tried this and realized that I could not pay the rent with lipstick sales. Still to this day I have boxes of unused cosmetics and body lotions sitting in my garage.

When Josh was close to two years old, I managed to find a part-time position as a solicitor's receptionist and hated every minute of it. The other staff were unfriendly, the phones would not stop ringing and unfortunately, the training was so lacking that I constantly felt out of my depth. I soon found myself a much more interesting and suitable position as an employment officer and trainer, assisting people in finding work. The one thing that really stands out about my time in this job was the people and the contacts I made.

So many of the unemployed individuals that took part in my three-week job search course found their feet and became highly successful business people. Many of them remembered me and how I didn't treat them any differently because of their situation. That respect and rapport paid off years later when I was trying to sell advertising and then real estate in the Cairns region. Always keep in mind how important it is to treat everyone equally!

By this stage, my marriage had run its course and I found myself a single mum with a toddler. It was a tough time in my life where I was renting a property, relying on public transport and constantly worried every time I went to pay for my groceries that there might not be enough money in my account. My job was also in doubt due to government funding changes. It was time to look for a new opportunity.

A human resources position become available on Green Island, just off the coast of Cairns. This was an amazing role and I got to travel across to one of the most scenic islands in the world every day. I have to say that as hard as we worked on the island, the staff also threw some amazing parties too! I had a couple of great years working in this position, but I found it was a tough role to be in with a young child to care for. It was while I working in this role on the Island that I happened to attend a seminar that changed my life forever!

It was a seminar for first-home buyers wanting to build their own home. I remember attending this seminar with my mum, thinking how nice it would be to one day build my own home. I never dreamed in a million years that I would receive a phone call a few days later from the mortgage broker who'd given me a form to fill in at the seminar, to tell me that I was qualified to get a home loan. At the time, the government was giving out generous amounts to first-home buyers to help with deposits. Without this assistance, I dread to think how long it would've taken me to jump into the real estate world.

This first home could not have been timed better in the real estate cycle in Cairns — the market was on the rise and less than a year after I built my first home, I was able to use the equity to buy an investment unit in the city. This unit also happened to be the very first unit that I listed on Airbnb… but I'll tell you more about that later.

My first investment property and also my first listing on Airbnb is a one-bedroom unit in this complex. We now have a second unit that we own listed on Airbnb at this location.

I took on managing the unit myself and quickly learned as much as I possibly could about property management. The rent on the unit was covering all expenses so I didn't have to put in a cent. Soon after, I was able to once again use the equity from the two properties to purchase another unit in Edge Hill. This property was a two-bedroom unit that I managed to secure for $105,000 and was bringing in enough income to cover its costs.

I was working on a formula for investment properties to identify if they would be positively geared (or close enough) so that I didn't have to put my hand in my pocket, which was a good thing as I was not making a great salary at the time. It was amazing that a single mum on a mediocre salary was able to collect a property portfolio, purely using the equity of other properties to secure more. I'm not sure the banks would be so generous these days.

The little Edge Hill unit that I purchased quickly grew in capital gains and only nine months after I purchased it, I made the decision to sell and made a quick $30,000 in profit. It astounded and excited me that I could make so much money from real estate in comparison to working a full-time job. Funnily enough, the current owner of this property has just listed this unit with my business as an Airbnb property — what a small world!

MY STORY | 25

We currently list the unit I previously owned on Airbnb on behalf of the current owner.

Over the next few years, I made two more key property purchases. The first one was close to home — the second, close to my heart.

My neighbors at Shamrock Avenue were looking to build a larger home and considering selling their current property. Over a few glasses of wine one night, on a scrap piece of paper, we wrote up a "contract" for me to purchase their home. It was a three-bed, one-bath home in a popular, family-friendly suburb of Cairns that would be an easy property to find tenants for. I rented this home to many family, friends and young couples starting out.

I get a real buzz out of purchasing an investment property that will not only reward me (that's always the plan) but also helps others. With this property purchase, my neighbors were able to save themselves the hassle of listing and selling their home through an agent who would've charged a commission. The purchase of this new house also changed the lives of many families who rented the home. It was so exciting to see four new babies born to various families over the years who will always know it as their first home.

Shamrock Avenue house that I long term lease… not Airbnb… want to know why?? Read on.

The second key house purchase that I made around this time looked foolish on paper but meant everything to me personally. I was in the financial position to really make an influence on others and in this case, it was to assist my grandparents.

Val and Norm Bell (my mother's parents) lived on Cameron Street in Inverell, New South Wales for as long as I could remember. My grandfather built the home himself and it was the one street address that was a constant in our family. It was the gathering spot for most Christmases and I have fond memories of sitting around the tree in the lounge room with my sisters and cousins, all guessing what was wrapped up amongst the pile of presents.

Pa would park himself at the end of the kitchen bench on a home-made stool (he was a gifted woodworker) sipping on Lambrusco while Nan would teach her grandchildren how to play card games. Living solely off the old-age pension didn't allow for any luxuries and it was always "budget, budget, budget" to make ends meet. It was through witnessing this struggle that I made them a proposal — for me to purchase their home.

Nan and Pa would then become tenants in their own home, paying a minimal rent to meet my expenses on the home but in turn, have more money at their disposal than they could ever have imagined. This was a proposal that my grandfather struggled to get his head around. As a proud man, he didn't ever want to be seen to be accepting charity, so I had to put all of my sales skills to the test so I could convince him it was a good property investment for me. I'm not sure if he ever bought this spiel, but he eventually agreed.

Unfortunately, they both passed away in quick succession, within seven years of this property purchase, but I am happy to say that they both had a very comfortable and enjoyable lifestyle in their later years. In 2016, it was time to sell the Cameron Street house and in a slow, flat real estate market (which I knew when I bought it) this was not an easy task, so I had to rent the home out while I waited for a buyer. The sale resulted in a financial loss for me, but it will always be remembered as a very worthwhile investment.

Cameron St, Inverell – my Grandparents home

Small Business and the Corporate World

As well as my property investments, I always had a million business ideas running through my head, but the timing and situation had to be just right to launch the concept I had for it to be successful. Josh was just starting school and was not enjoying being stuck in daycare before and after school while his mum was over on a tropical island each day. It was not an optimal situation, so the sale proceeds from the Edge Hill unit made it easier for me make the leap from working full-time to starting up my own business again.

I had an idea where I could shop for other people. I knew there was a target market of elderly people that could not easily get to the shops, busy business owners who did not have time to purchase birthday presents, party animals who needed someone to drive to McDonalds for them to collect dinner when they'd had too much to drink or even fishing charter boats who wanted to stock up for their next outing. There were so many opportunities for a shopping and errand service that I developed a business called Shop and Deliver. Years before Uber Eats or Coles Home Delivery, there was a demand — just not the services offering to go and get your meals or your shopping for you.

> **I always had a million business ideas running through my head**

There was one lady who would have me shop for her every second day as she was not physically able to leave her house and had no immediate family. Looking back on this situation now, I think she was lonely and employing me to run errands for her meant that she had companionship when I made her deliveries.

I quickly created a role for myself and brought in enough money to replace the salary from my previous job. What I struggled with (and didn't have the right skills for, at the time) was scaling up and growing the business. I had good intentions and willing casual workers, but I just didn't have a good plan in place to grow the business to sustain a team.

The cartoon logo trend continues

Julie and Josh in Shop and Deliver uniform

It was during this time that I met my current husband Mark, who as a logically thinking, reserved and cautious tradesman, complimented my outgoing nature and risk-taking attitude. It is a perfect balance that has seen our relationship last more than eleven years. Mark has taken on the role of more than a step-dad to Josh — Mark considers Josh to be his best mate.

A happy personal life put me in a great frame of mind to continue to try and grow my new shopping business. Marketing the business was very different to how it is done nowadays, so I designed an ad to place in the phonebook. I had developed a great relationship with the sales consultant of the local phonebook who, when it came time to deliver the phonebooks to every household in Cairns, suggested that my business might like to assist in this task.

I hired a couple of willing backpackers and we got to work delivering the books door-to-door. On completion of this task, it was put to me that perhaps I should come and work for the phonebook company. I laughed it off, but always one to keep options open, I attended the interview anyway to find out what all the fuss was about.

It took me about two minutes to decide to jump into this new career in advertising when it was explained that I could continue to run Shop and Deliver, but also take on duties to work on in my own time, selling advertising to businesses in the Cairns region. The money, flexibility, and attitude of this company really appealed to me.

It was not too long after I took on this role that I worked out my hourly income shopping for others was around $25 per hour, yet I could easily earn up to $100 per hour selling advertising. So, guess what I did — I closed the business down and concentrated on a job that I loved for almost a decade.

The company I was working for was a direct competitor to Yellow Pages. In Cairns, it was a much better value option, and highly popular as a result. Personally, I loved that the owners were entrepreneurial and willing to take a risk in a rapidly changing industry. Print advertising was quickly losing its appeal in the marketplace, with online advertising and smartphone apps taking over. This company was able to adapt and change to keep up with the demands of local business owners.

One of my greatest achievements during this time was to take on the rural Tablelands location, which did not have a dedicated phonebook and business owners relied on the North Queensland Yellow Pages as the only comprehensive directory they could advertise in. I was asked to take on a project to launch a phonebook in the area and that meant starting from scratch. I had to sell the dream to businesses in the area and convince them to take a risk, investing in a product that didn't yet exist. I sold over $200,000 of advertising space to business owners that year and we launched the inaugural Tablelands phonebook, which is still going today. At the annual company conference that year, I won the Sales Representative of the Year national award, an absolute highlight of my career.

Eventually, I was promoted to the position of sales performance manager, in charge of locations like Darwin, Alice Springs, Cairns, Townsville, and Mackay. This role meant traveling all over the country and ensuring local sales representatives had the training and tools needed to achieve sales budgets. It was hectic and financially rewarding but took a toll on my family life and health. I was away from home three weeks out of four, working ridiculous hours and an absolute slave to my phone. It was a role that I had strived to reach, and I loved the feeling of having achieved a major goal.

What I had not planned for was how the stress of the job was going to affect me and in 2015, I was diagnosed with adrenal burnout and breakdown. I went into a deep depression and couldn't function properly. My speech was affected, and I was bedridden for months. Unfortunately, I had to resign from my position and halt my crazy, fast-paced lifestyle.

I was very lucky that I had my supportive husband Mark by my side during this time. He was able to look after our finances, take on the role of a sole parent and assist me as I struggled through a terribly stressful and sad time in my life.

It took months of medication, meditation, massage, naturopathy, and any other kind of treatment I could find to try and regain my energy and sanity again. I realized (the hard way) that I needed to find balance in my life and be wary of how my stress levels would be affected in the future. During my recovery, I decided to change pace with my career and to take a slightly different direction. I started studying for my real estate certificate. I had always had an interest in real estate, so it made sense to try and combine my hobby with my sales background.

I was very fortunate to join a family-owned leading real estate agency in Cairns. The founder's grandson was the sales manager, who took me under his wing and taught me all about the world of real estate. Unfortunately, the market was not buoyant at the time I entered the field and it was bloody hard trying to get a sale across the line. I encountered many frustrated property owners who were looking for answers, tossing up whether to sell in a flat market or to rent out their homes to tenants in the hope that the market would pick up soon. Either option usually cost the owners money. What was missing in the marketplace was a third option, one that allowed property owners to use their own properties while receiving enough money to cover their expenses — that was until Airbnb hit Cairns.

Airbnb Turned My Life Upside Down

In March 2016, one of my tenants moved out of my one-bedroom unit in the city, giving me the opportunity to try out this new Airbnb phenomenon — what was all the fuss about?

I recognized the Cairns, Queensland Australia (where I live and have my properties) was the ideal location for Airbnb success – we have an international airport bringing in thousands of visitors keen to explore the Great Barrier Reef and the surrounding Rainforest. Cairns is also lacking enough traditional accommodation (hotels and holiday apartments) to keep up with the demand. At the time I decided to list my one-bedroom unit it was the 'perfect storm' to ensure Airbnb success.

After furnishing the property with a sofa bed (to sleep 4 guests), homewares, and connecting the internet and electricity in my name, I was soon able to welcome my first guests.

The benefits soon began to show and I increased my standard long-term rental income of $240 per week to an average of $600 per week by listing on Airbnb. Sure, there was a bit more work involved in hosting the property, but I also got to use the property myself which I had never had the opportunity to do before. It was such a great experience meeting some amazing visitors from all over the world. I was lucky to have the support of family and friends who assisted with the cleaning and copious amounts of laundry.

It dawned on me that if I was having such success with my unit, other property owners would probably love to see similar returns. This is exactly what occurred to me while dealing with a client looking to buy an investment property in Cairns, who faced challenges that helped me realize the potential of an Airbnb management business. This Sydney-based investor had contacted me while I worked at the real estate agency in Cairns, about a property I had advertised for sale. It was a small two-bedroom unit in a less-than-desirable location and the cheapest property on my books. She arranged an inspection and a few days later, I met her there to show her around. Which took about 45 seconds, it was so small.

> I increased my standard long-term rental income of $240 per week to an average of $600 per week by listing on Airbnb

The property did not impress and at this stage, most real estate agents would thank the lady for her time and be on their way. However, I decided to ask some questions about what she was looking for and her end goal. I was trying to find a problem that I could provide a solution for. Her problem was that she wanted a property to bring in more income than expenses and she had a very small budget of $130,000.

I told her I would source a property for her and "create" a positively geared property. I explained to this lady how successful my own Airbnb property was performing and the amazing returns I was getting from this platform. I convinced her that if we could find the right property in the right location, we could replicate the success of my own unit.

I then scoured all the listings in Cairns at the bottom-end of the price range and identified five properties that could work. The next day, I chauffeured the lady around to these properties as her "buyer's agent" and eventually, she found one that ticked her boxes. I negotiated a deal for her and collected a referral fee from the agent. This lady had to return to Sydney so we had identified a new problem.

How was she going to manage the process of setting up the property in preparation for hosting on Airbnb? It needed a full clean, new furniture, homewares, linen and an internet connection. She was concerned about the cost of making a return trip to Cairns to do this first-hand. I offered to do this for her after working hours and on the weekends. I negotiated a consultancy fee to do the clean, furniture shopping, multiple trips to Kmart and Bunnings and set up an internet connection. This took quite a few days to complete, but it looked fantastic once we'd finished and it was a lot of fun. The next step was also a challenge.

How was she going to manage the process of listing her property on Airbnb, meeting and greeting the guests and then cleaning the property when she wasn't living nearby? This was a no-brainer! I offered my services to act as her property manager and handle the whole process on her behalf. I charged a 25% fee on the accommodation rate, plus I kept any cleaning fees paid by the guests. The result was that I managed to identify three ways to make income in this transaction.

1. Buyer's agent referral fee
2. Consultancy fee to set up the property and listing
3. Management fee and cleaning fee

The most exciting part is the property was so successful that the lady called me less than a year later, asked me to find another property and repeat the process. This time, she didn't have to fly to Cairns. She told me what her budget was, and I purchased another property for her — which she has never seen — furnished, fitted it out and listed it on Airbnb!

There was a business opportunity staring me in the face! In mid-2016, I started furiously working on a business plan and marketing ideas to bring Host My Home, my Airbnb property management company, to fruition. I officially launched this unique, one-of-a-kind business in November 2016 and left my position at the real estate agency, which was probably one of the scariest times in my working life.

I had to make the business work to replace my full-time wage... eek! I panicked a little and quickly joined another real estate platform that allowed sales agents to sell as much or as little as they wanted. In hindsight, this was probably a waste of time and energy. I now know that rather than spreading yourself too thin and trying to juggle too many balls (sales and short-term rentals), it's better to focus on something you're good at. Cairns is also a small town. I wanted to work *with* other agents, complimenting their services, not be seen as a competitor. I decided to let the sales agent work go after completing a couple of quick sales. It did help fund the business, so it wasn't a complete waste of time.

Once I made the decision to put 100% of my effort into the Airbnb property management business, we were off and running! In the beginning, my daily job description included sourcing new properties, appraising them for "Airbnb-worthiness", furnishing and fitting out the properties, listing them on the website, answering guest inquiries, meeting and greeting, and cleaning... so much cleaning! My record was making 17 beds in a day. Seven days a week, I could be either found makings beds, unloading a washing machine or in Kmart buying homewares for the latest listed property.

When it came to searching for other new properties to add to my portfolio, I was willing to consider anything and everything to get my business going. I look back and cringe at some of the properties I agreed to manage in the early days, including a couple of small studio units in a building affectionately known to locals as "the crack house". There were an interesting bunch of long-term tenants that occupied this building who often attracted the attention of the local police force.

The saving grace of this property was that it was located on the main road between the airport and the city center. We were also lucky to have a property owner who was prepared to put money, time and effort into the units to ensure they had good wi-fi, Netflix and beautiful furnishings. Unfortunately, we couldn't control the neighbors and started to get reviews on Airbnb that tarnished my reputation. Eventually, I decided to give up managing these units. I couldn't allow negative reviews to affect my other properties and the business I was establishing. A guest's review of the property paints a picture – '*Good place to see the city, bus passes fairly regularly and it's convenient. Just the neighbors are a bit strange.*'—**Fabio March 2017**

Another bad decision at the time was to take on the management of a two-bedroom unit in another undesirable complex. There was a stabbing there only a couple of months earlier. I was determined that I could turn this property into a success, although there was something creepy about the property owner. We increased the rental return on the property from $150 per week to $380 per week, but the property owner was still not overly impressed and wouldn't spend a cent replacing curtains with holes in them or the door lock... that didn't lock. Once again, I made the decision to part ways with this property (and its strange owner) as it was not helping me build a profile on Airbnb that was going to attract new clients or guests. It was only recently that we heard the owner had taken on the management of the property himself and installed cameras inside the property to spy on guests!

Instead, we chose to partner with properties (and property owners) that we felt comfortable and confident working with. I thought finding clients would be my biggest challenge in this business, but I was wrong. Once we had established our website, placed a few articles in the local magazine and word had spread that there was a new property management concept in town, we had people lining up to get their properties appraised. In January 2017, we had 17 active listings on Airbnb, which grew to 62 by the end of the year.

One of the best parts of running an Airbnb property management business is the feedback and reviews that you get from guests. They're not always favorable, but I now have more than 2000 reviews. It's great to read through them and see how much the guests have loved the homes and services we have provided for them. It makes all the hard work worthwhile!

One of my favorite reviews is below -

Accuracy	★ ★ ★ ★ ★	Location	★ ★ ★ ★ ★
Communication	★ ★ ★ ★ ★	Check-in	★ ★ ★ ★ ★
Cleanliness	★ ★ ★ ★ ★	Value	★ ★ ★ ★ ★

Ashley
June 2018

The house was amazing. The check in was super easy and pain-less. We checked in late at night and Julie had ensured we had all instructions to enjoy the stay. This was the beginning to a great stay. The bedroom layout was PERFECT and exactly what states on the website. The kitchen amenities were spectacular, the shower - WOW. Just wicked. The backyard is stunning so if you are here for the weekend you get two days to soak up the beautiful backyard oasis. Everything about this house is AMAZING and you will not regret your stay here. Super accessible, communication between host was easy and I will definitely be choosing this house as my first pick WHENEVER I need to stay in Cairns. REGARDLESS. You will not be disappointed in this choice of BnB. WE LOVED EVERY BIT OF IT.

In February 2017, I recruited a Personal Assistant and in less than a year, her skill-set saw her promoted to Operations Manager of my business. It is amazing how, when you take a risk and invest in the right people, your business grows so quickly. In 2017, I made some incredible additional human resource investments (possibly ones that were not in the budget at the time) that, in turn, grew my business income to another level.

I truly believe in recruiting people that are more highly skilled than I am to assist me in achieving my goals. I know I am a very average cleaner, so I have recruited some of the best people I can find that have the necessary attention to detail, are fit and take ownership over properties to ensure we never get a bad review on cleanliness. I know I lack the time to visit every property regularly to make sure the standards are kept to a high level for maintenance and cleanliness, so I have recruited a lady to do this for me. I know I don't have the energy for property appraisals or the networking we need to continuously grow our property portfolio, so I have recruited the perfect social butterfly to represent my company. She brings in multiple new properties each week to be managed by Host My Home Pty Ltd.

I have a personal belief that if you treat your staff well and give them ownership of their jobs, you will see loyalty and hard work in return. Each of our property hosts (they are co-hosts to my listings on the Airbnb platform) are allocated a portfolio of properties dependent on their capabilities and own income desires. It is almost like a franchise being handed to them. They are given properties to look after, clean, and maintain. They will meet and greet guests, ensure their stay is as good as possible can be and then clean up after them. If there is any damage or missing items after a guest stays, property hosts relay this to the office so it can then be reported to Airbnb.

Just this weekend (July 2018) I assisted one of my property hosts with cleaning as she had two large houses to turn around in the one day. What struck me during the time I spent with her was the pride she took in her job and the systems she had developed to get the job done. Her standards were much higher than I could ever had hoped for and we all had a laugh when she took one look at the bed I had just made, shook her head and promptly stripped it to 'start again'. She was not afraid to show the boss (me) that my bed making was sub-standard and needed to be redone. After hours of working when I felt we 'were done' my colleague was not 100% happy and pulled out the garden blower to 'tidy up' the patio and garden areas. How lucky am I to have people like this on my team??

Our property hosts can take on a portfolio of a couple of properties that will earn them a few hundred dollars each week, or they may decide to grow their portfolio to a massive level, where they then can have a team of cleaners underneath them to assist with their workload. It's hugely gratifying for me to watch others achieve their goals as a direct result of a decision I made to start this business.

My son Joshua worked as a property host for me for a short period when he was 19 and I will never forget the first time I asked him to meet and greet some guests at one of the units we manage. The guests were a couple of young marines from a US Navy ship in town for some fun. They asked Josh where they could buy alcohol, so he took them to the local bottle shop. From there, he took them out on the town to the local nightclubs, introduced them to the local women and partied hard with them for three days! Needless to say, we got a five-star review from those guests for offering such great hospitality.

One of the goals I had with the business was to have a dedicated office space to work from. A year after we started the business, we moved into the only known dedicated Airbnb property management office in Australia. Before this, we were operating from my spare bedroom at home and an investment property that my husband and I had empty for a few months. Just as the business took off from investing in the right staff, it boomed when we found the right premises to operate from. Suddenly, with a professional image portrayed by an office space fitted out with a boardroom, reception area, staff room and amazing signage on the exterior, our business inquiries went crazy. The new office gave our business credibility, the public saw stability and the marks of our business success shone through.

Essentially, we had to establish our "one-of-a-kind" business with all the licensing and audit requirements that come with it in Queensland. Setting up a trust account and looking for computer software that would recognize Airbnb bookings wasn't the easiest task, but we have now formulated a business structure that allowed us to continue to grow into one of Australia's leading Airbnb property management companies. Our business structure has adapted since we have started so we can "work smarter, not harder".

At one stage, when we were working 'harder not smarter', I thought it was a good idea to do all the laundry ourselves. We set up our office space so that we had our desks right next to commercial washing machines and piles of linen that needed folding. Unfortunately, the linen took over from the day-to-day running of the business and distracted from our goal of growing the property portfolio. Instead of prospecting for new clients, we were too busy putting a load of washing on, hanging it out or trying to figure out the best way to fold a fitted sheet. Sorting the laundry in-house didn't save us any money in the long run, so the process was changed and the business works much better for it. Besides, I still can't fold a fitted sheet properly.

In the beginning, the main service that we offered at Host My Home was a "full management" option, where homeowners gave us complete control of their property and we would take care of the cleaning, maintenance, guest inquiries, meeting the guests and even putting the rubbish bins out every week. For this service, we charge a commission on the accommodation income, plus we charge each guest a cleaning fee.

As the business grew, so did our range of services. I was open to being flexible and working to find solutions to the challenges our clients faced. We took on quite a few "babysitting" jobs for established Airbnb hosts that needed a break themselves. We would set a minimum timeframe of a month on these jobs and charge either commission plus a cleaning fee or an hourly rate, depending on what the situation required.

Another service that we offered was to furnish and fit out properties for owners who didn't have the time or capabilities to do it themselves. We would estimate a budget, discuss design ideas and colors, and then go shopping to get the property "Airbnb-ready". This is one of the services that most of my friends and family comment on being a dream job — shopping with someone else's money. We have become very familiar with some of the large furniture shops and homeware outlets in the Cairns region. We also know to avoid flat-pack furniture and the dreaded Allen keys like the plague! We charge an hourly rate for this service and it often surprises our clients how quickly we can get the task completed.

We also offer a consultation service, charged at an hourly rate, to help people list their own properties and train them in the best way to operate their Airbnb accounts. There is a huge market for homeowners wanting to host their properties but needing a little guidance to get on the right track. A lot of people will say it is crazy to give away your secrets but quite honestly, there is enough work to go around and if it is not to a local business in direct competition with us, then I am happy to share my expertise. We have helped others trying to build up similar businesses in Australia and overseas — a number of business owners in the USA and Canada have reached out to us for advice.

Mel and Nadja from Team BnB in Noosa were establishing their own Airbnb property management business in 2017 and contacted me to see if I could give them some tips and pointers. We worked together over the phone to talk about business structure, accounting systems, website layout, co-hosting structures, and more. I am happy to say that I learned just as much from these girls as they learned from me. They are now the leading Airbnb property management company in their local area and I could not be prouder!

Another target market for consultations was the hotel and holiday unit market, where there are people who have paid millions of dollars for the management rights of a property. Prior to the introduction of Airbnb, this was an attractive business model, where you could buy the management rights of a property and individual property owners would appoint you to manage their unit. Once Airbnb was introduced, property owners were attracted to the cheaper option of becoming instant hotel managers themselves or even appointing an outside property management company such as Host My Home to list their property on Airbnb. The returns of Airbnb were often a lot more attractive, while the costs were less.

In mid-2017, we were contacted by a management rights owner asking for help — training to list and manage a property on Airbnb. The property owner of this unit was threatening to take it out of their pool to list independently on Airbnb. This on-site manager had the foresight that if she did not learn how to operate the Airbnb platform quickly, she may lose not only this unit but possibly her whole business.

Host My Home worked with this lady and consulted her on how to furnish and decorate the unit appropriately for Airbnb guests. We then arranged professional photographs of the property and created her profile and listing on Airbnb. Once everything was in place, we sat with her for quite a few hours to train her on how to answer inquiries, sync her calendar with her own holiday booking system and work her pricing so she could optimize her occupancy. For the first few weeks, we acted as a co-host on her listing, so that we could assist if she needed us. I am now happy to report she has achieved "super host" status and has recently listed her second unit.

If more on-site managers can train up on Airbnb and learn how to operate the platform, it might be a new service they can offer to owners and, in turn, retain their pool of properties. Another service we began to offer in 2017 was to act as a booking agent. This is a service we offer when the owner of a property is confident in meeting and greeting guests and doing the cleaning but is completely terrified or unable to operate the Airbnb software.

One of our first booking agent clients was a property based at Lake Tinaroo (approximately an hour away from Cairns), where the owners already had a great cleaner in place and a lock-box allowing guests to gain entry without any intervention from our client. What they needed was for someone to list the property on Airbnb, monitor the bookings and respond to guest inquiries. Host My Home was more than happy to take care of this for the owner.

After initially inspecting the property to get a good understanding of the amenities and the location of the home, we could easily answer inquiries and encourage bookings from guests on Airbnb. When a booking takes place, we simply inform the owner as to when they can expect guests. We charge a percentage of the nightly rate as a booking agent fee and invoice them at the end of the month. Up until August 2018 we were able to arrange a 'co-host' split through the Airbnb platform, but due to software changes this option is not longer available.

The success of the return-on-investment for our property owners has resulted in many of them asking us to source and assist in the purchasing of more investment properties for them. One of my team is a registered real estate agent and knows where to locate the best-performing Airbnb properties to buy for our clients. Once we establish the client's budget, desired location, and property size, we go out to search through listings to identify the best purchasing opportunities for them. Once we find a winner, we negotiate on behalf of the purchaser. The more money we can save the investor, the better!

We have seen some amazing success stories during our journey, such as a granny flat that was sitting mostly unused. The owners wanted to see if it could make them some residual income and it turned out to be extremely popular.

Some of our Success Stories -

PROPERTY	BEFORE AIRBNB	AIRBNB RETURNS
2 Bed / 1 Bath Granny Flat in Edge HilliHHill	Attached to a home this was only used for relatives to stay in	$700 per week on average

PROPERTY	BEFORE AIRBNB	AIRBNB RETURNS
6 Bed / 3 Bath home on the City fringe catering for large groups	The property was leased to long term tenants at approximately $600 per week	$1217 per week on average. In July 2018 the owner received $2000 per week after management fees were deducted.

The opportunities appear to be endless with the popularity and constant development of Airbnb. It is hard to predict how my Airbnb property management business will look five years from now, but we have set ourselves up to be flexible enough so that we can focus on our main goal — to make our property owners as big an ROI as possible.

Over the past 18 months we have listed approximately 143 properties on Airbnb. Around 100 of these are active at any one time (with owners sometimes pausing their listing if they decide to use it personally for a while).

Host My Home now employs a large team of people in the Cairns region and we have more work that we can keep up with flowing through the door. The business is now established so that I can work *on* it, not *in* it. It has given me the financial and personal freedom to live the lifestyle I had always dreamed of. I am not tied to a 9-to-5 job or answering to a boss, I have an awesome team of staff who can run

MY STORY | 49

the business while I am traveling and spending time with my family. In fact, I am writing this now from the Tip of Cape York where we are on yet another adventure. I have just returned from Bali and next week we go to the Gold Coast for a few days. Life is good! Now, I would like to share my tips and show you different methods for making your own income off the back of the sharing economy.

Here is a sample of the Airbnb listings under Julie's management –

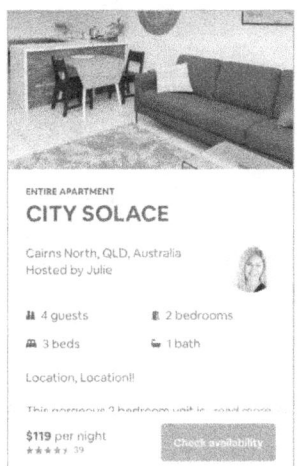

50 | MILLION DOLLAR HOST

ENTIRE HOUSE
Ideal Holiday Home in Beautiful Trinity Beach!
Trinity Beach, QLD, Australia
Hosted by Julie

- 6 guests
- 2 bedrooms
- 4 beds
- 2.5 baths

Tucked into a lovely, quiet street, this

$180 per night
★★★★★ 18   Check availability

ENTIRE APARTMENT
Spectacular Resort Living - 3km to City & Airport
Cairns North, QLD, Australia
Hosted by Julie

- 4 guests
- 2 bedrooms
- 3 beds
- 1 bath

$130 per night
★★★★★ 11   Check availability

ENTIRE HOUSE
Whitfield Luxury, Beautiful Home in the Tropics!!
Whitfield, QLD, Australia
Hosted by Julie

- 11 guests
- 5 bedrooms
- 6 beds
- 3 baths

$225 per night
★★★★★ 16   Check availability

ENTIRE APARTMENT
Spectacular Resort Living - 3km to City & Airport
Cairns North, Queensland, Australia
Hosted by Julie

$129 per ni...
★★★★★ 17   Check availability

ENTIRE APARTMENT
Affordable Luxury Accomodation on City Outskirts!
Cairns North, Queensland, Australia
Hosted by Julie

$109 per ni...
★★★★½ 26   Check availability

ENTIRE HOUSE
Clifton Retreat - Gigantic Pool - Family Friendly
Clifton Beach, Queensland, Australia
Hosted by Julie

$200 per ni...
★★★★★ 35   Check availability

Airbnb Basics

What is Airbnb?

Airbnb is an online platform that allows millions of homeowners across the world to list and lease their own personal space to travelers. One of the most successful businesses in the "sharing economy", Airbnb is now a billion-dollar company operating from its headquarters in San Francisco. It was founded in 2008 by Brian Chesky, Joe Gebbia and Nathan Blecharczyk, three young guys who discovered an amazing niche market, just trying to make some extra money to cover their rent by listing an air mattress on the floor of their living room. Their attempt at turning their home into an instant bed-and-breakfast was so successful that they ended up launching what is now a worldwide phenomenon!

> **One of the most successful businesses in the "sharing economy", Airbnb is now a billion-dollar company**

So, no matter who you are or what kind of background you have, you can now become an instant hotel manager. Airbnb gives you complete control over how much time you want to put into this new role, the "house rules" you will put in place, the kinds of travelers you are willing to accept and how much interaction you would like with your guests.

Whether the space you want to rent out is a spare room in your house, a granny flat in your backyard or an investment property, you can list it on Airbnb. I have seen treehouses, boats, igloos, and tents listed for travelers to stay in. Having people stay in your home is not a new concept by any means — couch-surfing has been around for decades. What is new and exciting is the online platform and the systems Airbnb has in place to make having guests a safe, trusted and positive experience.

Airbnb offers a great support system to assist you with the logistics of hosting and also offers insurance for guest damages and liability coverage. Airbnb will also collect upfront payment so, no need to worry about billing or chasing money. This is designed to give you peace of mind when welcoming guests into your home. Guest screening is also very stringent and to make a booking on Airbnb, a guest must verify their identity. Phone numbers and email addresses are also checked and verified.

The review system is the most amazing part of the Airbnb system. It's what keeps both hosts and guests honest and brings out the best in humanity through an attempt to strive to impress each other, to achieve a good review. They're only visible when both the guest and the host have completed each other's reviews, so there's no waiting to see what the other person has said about you before reviewing them — it's an honest appraisal. It is because of this clever system that guests will be on their best behavior and stick to the house rules, cleaning up after themselves and not stealing anything that isn't pinned down. Can you imagine a hotel guest respecting their surroundings in the same way?

Airbnb is simply an amazing online booking platform and stands heads and shoulders above other booking sites. I am often asked by property owners why I use Airbnb exclusively. I have tried the other sites and they just don't compare. Airbnb collects payments for you, offer a guarantee for damages or breakages caused by guests, offer a 24-hour helpline and are always updating their model to stay ahead of competitors. The Airbnb system is well-thought-out, easy to use, moves with the times and guests are an absolute joy to host!

How Can Airbnb Change Your Life?

Now that you know what Airbnb is, let me show you a few basic ways that you can get started. All the options below can be listed on Airbnb, but the chance of them being successful will depend on the location, facilities, marketing, and pricing.

Not all homes are suitable for Airbnb and you will need to do an assessment on your property before deciding to take the plunge to list your space.

You may be surprised to know that only three of the five investment properties my family owns are listed on Airbnb. Two of these properties are houses in the outer suburbs of Cairns and to furnish and fit-out the properties would be too expensive for the return I believe could be achieved on Airbnb. The two homes not listed on Airbnb do not offer a pool or anything special, so the nightly rate that I would charge to guests would have to be extremely low. I believe the most optimal strategy for ROI (return on investment) is to long term lease these properties.

The three properties that are listed on Airbnb and owned by my husband and I, are situated in the city centre and are occupied by Airbnb guests a minimum of 5 nights a week. We have the luxury of using these properties ourselves when we want and when they do have guests in them they are bringing in a great income for us.

The locations that do attract a lot of inquiries on Airbnb are usually those that are close to tourist attractions, airports, city centers, convention centers, beaches, and lakes. I have listed properties in suburbs that are too far away from the action and the occupancy on those places is very low. The owners of these properties decided to list on Airbnb mainly to earn a small amount of income while having the freedom to use the property themselves.

> The owners of these properties decided to list on Airbnb mainly to earn a small amount of income while having the freedom to use the property themselves.

The facilities of a property also impact its success. Those properties that are unique, such as homes in the rainforest or places that have a resort-style pool are very popular with guests. If you can offer the latest in technology, like unlimited and super-fast wi-fi, smart TVs in all bedrooms, a pool table and a games room, you can also expect that the property will get booked out quickly.

The marketing of the property includes having professional photos, floorplans (rare to see these on listings but they attract a *lot* of inquiries), a detailed description and a comprehensive listing on Airbnb. Once the listing has gone live, there is also the opportunity to push the link through your own website or social media avenues. Let your family and friends know that your "instant hotel" has opened for business.

Pricing is where a lot of people come unstuck. I see too many property owners getting greedy, believing that their home is worth more than guests believe it is… and it sits empty. Please don't think that all of the properties you see on Airbnb are being booked enough to be turning a profit — most are sitting vacant. Research your market before setting your prices and then use the smart pricing algorithm on Airbnb. It will increase or decrease your pricing according to demand at the time in your location.

Please be aware that Airbnb is constantly updating or changing their systems, policies and procedures. What you are reading today is current in 2018, but you will need to get updated information if you are reading this a few years from now.

So, let's look at a few ways that Airbnb can dramatically change your life and your bank balance.

Rent a Room in Your House

One of the best ways to explore the Airbnb platform is to start in your own home. Perhaps you have a spare room in your house or a granny flat sitting empty in the backyard? Airbnb now offers the perfect platform to turn these spare rooms into extra income that might just mean you don't have to take on that second job or work overtime any longer. If there is a space where travelers can lay their head, you're sitting on a potential goldmine.

You will have to be prepared to share common spaces such as the lounge room, kitchen, and patios with visitors in your home. This might be quite a culture shock for some homeowners, so consider this very seriously before committing. On the listing, you need to be very specific about boundaries and point out exactly what the guests can expect before they turn up on your doorstep. If you don't want guests to park their car in your garage, you are going to have to specifically write that "parking is on-street only".

> **If there is a space where travelers can lay their head, you're sitting on a potential goldmine.**

You must also be very specific about the use of wi-fi as some guests will expect to have unlimited access and may spend all day downloading movies which could use up your data allowance if you have a capped broadband package. If you are happy to share a meal with your guests, write this into the description and let them know if there are any extra charges if they take up the offer of dinner. As much as you want to set boundaries, your guests will want the same respect — they are paying for their own privacy.

When setting up the listing on Airbnb, you will be asked a *lot* of questions about your home including shared spaces, wi-fi set up, private entries, whether there is a private bathroom for guests to use and if linen is included. Please take the time to fully answer all questions and check your listing completely before you activate it online. It only takes one little mistake for your new guest to turn up on your doorstep with no notice… because you forgot the section on "instant bookings with no notice needed".

The Pros

- You will make money.
- You will make lots of new friends from all over the world.
- Your spare room will produce enough income for you to give up your second job or cut back your hours at work.

The Cons

- Strangers will be staying in your home and sharing your common spaces.
- Your personal space may be invaded.
- You will be expected to entertain, even on days that you want to sit around in your underwear on the couch.

Rent Out Your Home While You Are on Holidays

The traditional solution when you go on holiday is to ask a friend, relative or neighbor to care for your house while you're away. An alternative is to pay someone to do it for you or get a house-sitter to stay at your place. Unfortunately, there wasn't really a solution for paying the bills while you sipped cocktails on a tropical beach… until now.

Listing your home on Airbnb and engaging a co-host or professional management company to "babysit" your listing while you're away may not only bring in extra money while you travel but it may mean you can extend your travel plans to stay away for longer.

> There wasn't really a solution for paying the bills while you sipped cocktails on a tropical beach... until now.

One of my favorite examples of how this can work so well was a couple who had Host My Home manage their property for a few months while they went overseas on the trip of a lifetime. The house was in the outer suburbs of Cairns, a wooden pole home surrounded by rainforest without any typical attractions such as a pool. Realistically, this couple was engaging our services to ensure that their home was looked after while they were away and that someone could manage the gardening, check security, water their plants and perhaps make them a little bit of money to cover their bills while they traveled.

I remember making a joke before they left that if we did make a decent amount from the property that they could just "keep traveling"… well, guess what happened? The house was super-popular on Airbnb, bringing in a constant return of $700 (after our fees were deducted) for the home-owners. Guests were attracted to the unique nature of the home and the opportunity to see Australian wildlife up close. I remember the excitement of writing emails to the homeowners to let them know about the flow of bookings and how I needed them to keep traveling. Which they did, extending their trip by a few more weeks!

I have also seen people take holidays who would never have been able to do so before, using the income they are making on their Airbnb properties. A single mother who worked as a teacher's aid asked me to manage her property for six weeks in 2017. She calculated that with her income from Airbnb bookings, she could not only pay her mortgage, rates and electricity bill, but she could also afford to visit her family interstate for the first time in years! So, what are the pros and cons of renting your house out while you are on holiday?

The Pros

- You will make money.
- As guests are vetted, you know only recommended guests are accepted.
- Airbnb offers a 'Host Guarantee' to cover any damage to your personal property.
- The security of your home will be increased with people staying there.
- Your home will be professionally cleaned and maintained on a regular basis.

The Cons

- Strangers will be staying in your home and sleeping in your bed.
- Your appliances and furniture will be used (I would recommend you lock up any personal items you don't want to be touched).
- There are no guarantees that bookings will coincide with your holidays.
- Your neighbors may be affected by guest noise, arrival, departure, etc.

Rent Out Your Investment Property

Have you got an investment property with a long-term tenant in it? Perhaps it is not performing as well as you would like it to financially, or maybe you would like to have the freedom to use the property yourself. Imagine being able to stay in your own investment property whenever you want instead of having to ensure you have to have a tenant at all times in order to meet your financial repayments on the property.

> **Imagine being able to stay in your own investment property whenever you want instead of having to ensure you have to have a tenant at all times in order to meet your financial repayments on the property.**

If the property is located close to the city center, tourist attractions, convention centers or offers amazing views, it will most likely be well-sought-after by Airbnb travelers. You can research this by looking on the site or consulting third-party websites like AirDNA to see how many other properties are listed and what type of income they're producing.

The beauty of Airbnb is that you can list your property ahead of time to see if it works. For example, you may not have tenants moving out of your investment property for a few weeks but there is nothing stopping you from listing the property ahead of time (if you have good photos), keeping the calendar blocked until your tenants have departed. If your tenants have nice furniture, you could always ask permission to photograph the home with their furniture in it and make it known in the description on Airbnb that the property has been newly refurbished, and the furniture will be slightly different once the guests arrive.

This allows you to see how many people inquire and book your property. I have used this method a couple of times with properties we were not 100% sure of and it worked well in getting advance bookings. You will need to check your body corporate and local council laws in relation to using the property for short-term leasing. You will also need to check your home insurance to ensure it covers paying guests staying at your property.

The Pros

- You will make money.
- You will be able to stay in your own investment property if you need to.
- Your property will probably be better-maintained and cleaned more regularly than if it was being leased long-term.

The Cons

- It is quite an expensive exercise to set up a property to be "Airbnb-ready".
- There are no guarantees of occupancy and there is a risk that your property may sit empty.
- You will have to check insurance policies and body corporate rulings to ensure your investment property is meeting all regulations.

Buy Yourself a Holiday Home

Imagine purchasing a property in your dream holiday destination and staying in it every year, knowing that it's not costing you a cent! What if, by listing this home on Airbnb, you could not only cover the property costs but have the holiday home of your dreams?

Firstly, you need to find a property that appeals to you (and other holidaymakers) and get an appraisal done by a professional Airbnb property management company to ensure that demand and occupancy are high enough to make this a successful investment.

> What if, by listing this home on Airbnb, you could not only cover the property costs but have the holiday home of your dreams?

You will then want to engage a full-time property manager to manage the logistics of running the property as a holiday home for you and make sure it is regularly cleaned while earning maximum income throughout the peak season.

When you are looking at income, make sure you are covering all the annual expenses of the property including rates, insurances, and mortgage repayments. The most appealing part about this whole arrangement is that you — the property owner — will get to holiday in your property and it won't cost you a cent.

So, does it work? It has for these happy property owners, who can now own a holiday home and have travelers pay off their expenses!

Laguna On Spence

Great, little one-bedroom unit that was purchased in 2016.

The refurbishment cost to make it Airbnb-ready – $3,500.

The yearly costs for the first year including mortgage repayments*, council rates, body corporate fees, electricity, wi-fi, and maintenance has totaled – $15,836.

The average return via Airbnb has been $479 per week totaling – $24,908

First-year profit – $5,572 / Predicted future yearly profit – $9,072

Cairns City Apartment

One-bedroom, executive-style unit with fold-out sofa lounge, to sleep four people.

The refurbishment cost to make it Airbnb-ready – $5,500.

The yearly costs for the first year including mortgage repayments*, council rates, body corporate fees, electricity, wi-fi, and maintenance has totaled – $18,551.

The average return via Airbnb has been $582 per week totaling – $30,264

First-year profit – $6,213 / Predicted future yearly profit – $11,713

All figures quoted in this article are indicative only and Host My Home Pty Ltd does not guarantee any particular return or level of income.

*Mortgage repayments are calculated on a 20% deposit, 4% interest and a 25-year term.

The Pros

- You will make money and be able to pay off your dream holiday home.
- If you like to holiday in a particular destination, surely others feel the same way, so it should be popular.
- Your property will be cleaned and maintained on a regular basis, so when you use it there will be nothing to do but put your feet up.

The Cons

- The times you want to holiday may clash with the peak season — and you won't be making money while you're staying there.
- There are no guarantees of occupancy and there is a risk that your property may sit empty.
- You will have all your friends and family wanting to holiday at your property.

LET'S GET STARTED...
Creating A Listing & Making The Most Of It!

Essentials for Setting Up an Airbnb Property

Airbnb properties need to be fully-furnished and self-contained but there are no set standards and this is where many hosts find themselves being criticized in public reviews for a property not featuring the essentials or lacking certain household items.

Quite often, we will receive inquiries from guests asking if linen is included or if the kitchen has a rice cooker. You will need to accurately describe your home in the listing and if you need to include photos of kitchen appliances to meet the market, then do so.

> **Airbnb properties need to be fully-furnished and self-contained.**

You also need to provide quality, functional household goods if you want your property to be a success. One of the biggest costs for homeowners is linen and updating pillows to a good standard. We're often asked what color linen to provide and once again, there are no set rules. White linen is well-received by guests as it shows that there are no stains. However, there is a higher cost associated with the turnover of white linen.

Most towns have linen hire companies, but please be aware that this service can be quite costly and will eat into your profits very quickly. The one absolute *essential* when listing a property on Airbnb is to provide *free* and *unlimited* internet for your guests. It is as important to travelers as a comfortable bed. There are many providers now who offer unlimited internet packages with no contract. It's well worth the investment!

When we take on a new property we suggest that property owners provide the following items in their home as a minimum.

Bedrooms

- Two sets of sheets (we recommend 500 thread count) per bed, including sofa beds
- Mattress protector for each bed
- Pillows with protectors for each bed — two per person. We recommend the best pillows you can afford to ensure good reviews. Pillows need to be replaced regularly
- Bedcover — two per bed
- Bedside lamps
- Coat hangers — 10 per wardrobe
- Power points for charging devices

Bathrooms

- Two bath towels per guest
- Two pool towels per guest

- Two face towels per bathroom
- Two hand towels per bathroom
- Two bath mats per bathroom
- One waste paper basket per bathroom
- One toilet brush per toilet
- Hairdryer

Living Area

- Enough seating for the maximum number of occupants
- Cushions/throws/artwork and other decorative items
- Smart TV
- Internet — we recommend fast, reliable and unlimited

General

- Broom, dustpan and brush, mop and bucket
- Iron and ironing board
- Drying rack/pegs
- Vacuum cleaner
- Spray & Wipe or similar/general cleaning items for guests to use
- Bug spray

Kitchen

- Oven, microwave, fridge, and dishwasher
- Four sponges/dishcloths
- Two pairs of oven mitts
- At least five tea towels
- Three saucepans with lids, including a large one for pasta
- At least one frying pan

- Barbecue tools/utensils/cleaning apparatus
- Acrylic/plastic glasses for pool areas and children
- Casserole dishes/baking trays — we recommend one rectangular and one round
- Dinner plates, bowls, small plates, cups, water glasses, wine glasses — enough for the number of maximum occupants
- Toaster and kettle
- Rice cooker — very popular with our guests
- Sandwich toaster
- Dish rack
- Bottle opener
- Can opener
- Spatula and cooking spoons
- Salad and serving bowls
- Cutlery and steak knives — enough for the maximum number of occupants
- Colander
- Cutting knives and boards — we recommend at least two
- Plastic storage containers
- Measuring cups and spoons
- Tongs
- Vegetable peeler

Optional extras that may encourage more bookings

- Placemats, table runners
- DVD player
- Netflix/Austar/Foxtel subscription
- Games console
- Umbrella

- Torch and spare batteries
- Esky and camp chairs
- Pool toys/beach items
- Barbecue and gas bottle
- Kids' games
- Books/magazines
- First-aid kit
- Fire extinguisher

It's a nice touch to have a welcome letter prepared for your guests that outlines the property features such as parking spaces, security codes, wi-fi passwords, instructions for the remote, etc. List your mobile number so they can contact you with any concerns.

A map of the local area pointing out the closest convenience store, bottle shop, takeaway and even your favorite restaurant can also be a great help. If you can access a tourist brochure on your city (usually available at information centers or tour booking places) visitors will appreciate that information too. Guests coming to stay at your property are going to look to you as the local expert and ask your opinion on tourist attractions, restaurants to eat in, places to shop and events to attend.

There may be an opportunity to partner up or come to an arrangement with local providers to get a kick-back for any guest referrals you provide. One restaurant that I know of has a referral system set up where they give hosts a bunch of cards offering a discount for their guests. On the back of these cards is a code that identifies the host as the referral source. When 10 guests eat at the restaurant, the host is then sent a voucher for a free meal!

Another kickback opportunity may lie with your local tour desk or day tour operator. Once again, if the host refers business to them, a commission might be paid. Make sure that you are genuinely referring to companies that you would use, even if they're not giving you a kickback, or you may find that you are called out in a guest review for giving dodgy advice, which might harm your credibility on Airbnb. Would that be worth a free meal? No.

There is a reason guests have chosen to book a trip via Airbnb and not a hotel website — they want accommodation with character! Make your property homely and give it personality with some homely charms (wall prints, fresh flowers, books, etc.).

Consumables and Gifts for Guests

You will need to provide the following consumables for your guests as well, keep them topped up and make sure enough is provided for the number of guests and length of time they are staying at your property. There is nothing worse than running out of toilet paper on the second day of your week-long stay!

- Salt, pepper, oil, glad wrap, paper towel, and aluminum foil
- Coffee, tea, sugar, and milk
- Water — bottled or a jug in the fridge
- Basic cleaning supplies – cleaning spray, sponges, washing-up liquid, dishwasher tablets, rinse aid, washing powder, garbage bags, toilet cleaner
- Insect-repelling surface spray
- Toilet paper and tissues
- Soaps, shampoo, and conditioner

When I first started my Airbnb journey, I went a little over-the-top with consumables, providing mini shampoos, conditioners, body wash, lotions, and soaps. I liked the idea that I was running my own hotel and wanted to replicate the feeling of a five-star set-up. Along with the toiletries, I decided that guests would only want to book my property if I provided an awesome mini-bar too, so I spent about $20 on each guest, stocking the fridge with cans of soft drink, chips, chocolate, and all sorts of goodies.

> **There is nothing worse than running out of toilet paper on the second day of your week-long stay!**

The guests *did* love all these extras and left some awesome reviews, but I learned that I could save myself a lot of money, yet still achieve great guest responses. I now provide large, pump-bottle shampoos, conditioners, and body wash, which guests tend to prefer as there isn't a limited amount for them to use, and it also saves the cleaning of individual soap bars and packaging from the miniature hotel products I was using before.

Likewise, we cut back on the food and drinks we leave for guest — it hasn't hurt our reviews, but we saved a lot of money doing so. We ensure guests have tea, coffee, sugar, milk and either a packet of nice biscuits, chocolates or chips as a welcome gift. It is so rare to get anything for free these days, so a nice bottle of wine or a box of chocolates on arrival always tends to set the right mood for guests coming into a holiday apartment. This is certainly not essential, but a few dollars spent on a nice basket of fruit will go a long way towards a positive review from your guests and, in turn, repeat business!

Recently, we stopped providing a 600ml bottle of water for each guest, instead leaving a nice carafe of water in the fridge. This was a suggestion made to me by a member of my team which has saved us money, helped lower the amount of plastic waste and once again, not affected our guest reviews in any way. Just be sure to point out gifts for guests when they check in — a lot of people will think it's too good to be true that these lovely things are for them!

Steps to a Successful Listing

Now you have set up your property, let's go through the steps to creating and working your Airbnb listing.

STEP 1: Photography and Description

> **Most listings don't accurately reflect how fantastic properties are due to poor photography.**

The first step to creating an Airbnb listing is to take photos of your space. Most listings don't accurately reflect how fantastic properties are due to poor photography. Airbnb offers a free professional photography service in some areas. If it's available to you, Airbnb will send a photographer to your house to capture the best light, angles, and features. Please note that if you take Airbnb up on this service, the company holds the rights to the photos. If the service isn't available in your area, please consider seeking the services of a professional photographer — it will be worth the investment!

There is no limit on the number of photos you can add to your profile, but I would recommend you include…

Bedrooms – Photograph all sleeping areas and do whatever you can to make the beds look comfortable. Perhaps add some extra cushions or throw rug.

Bathrooms – Make sure they're clean and well-lit.

Kitchen – Guests will want detailed photos. Show off the appliances that your guests will be able to use during their stay.

Loungeroom – Capture the living areas of the home to show there is enough seating for the number of guests staying, plus the TV and other entertainment offerings.

Laundry – This is one of the most important rooms for an Airbnb guest.

Patio/entertaining area – Perhaps you could dress this area with a bottle of champagne or set the table to entice future guests into booking your property.

Outside image – Show guests what the property looks like from the outside. Even if your home is an ugly duckling, it's best to offer an accurate image for guests.

Local area – Some photographers may even be able to capture an aerial image of your home using a drone, showing proximity to the beach, tourist attractions and shops.

Floor plan – If you're able to, uploading a floor plan will attract bookings as guests *love* to know how properties are laid out and imagine where their kids might be sleeping in relation to themselves when booking a holiday home.

Be creative with your photos. Some of the catchiest lead photos feature collages, starbursts, arrows or wording. Below are examples of some that we use to grab the attention of guests.

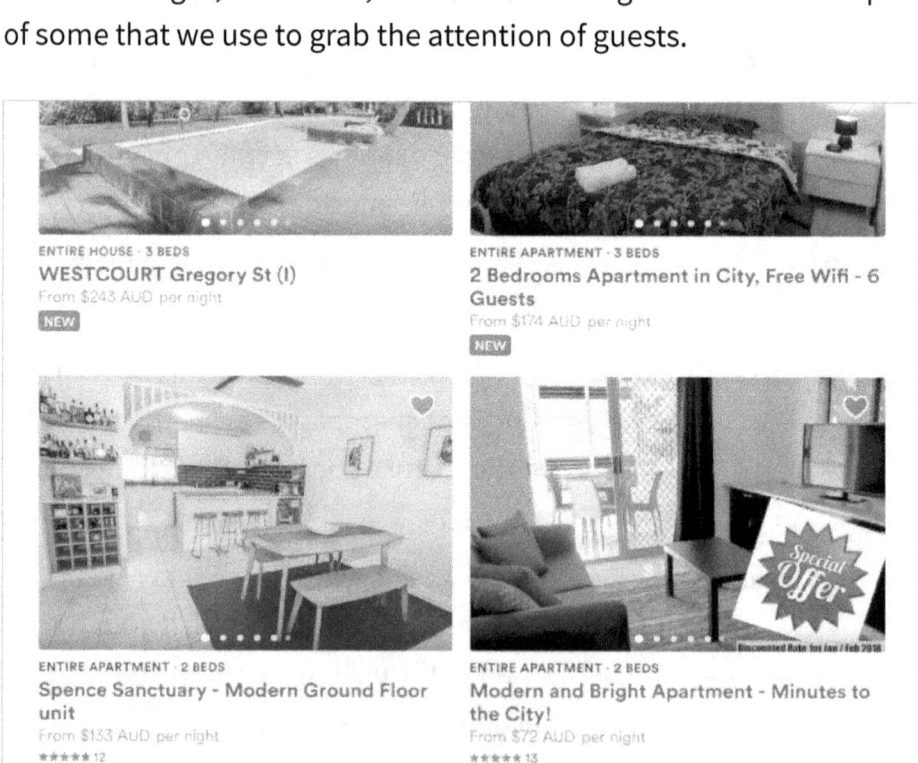

Be creative with adding wording to your photos or in this case a star burst offering a 'Special Offer'

Be as descriptive as you can when you are entering information into the Airbnb system. The process is very easy to follow and will prompt you by asking questions such as, "Tell me how many beds there are?" and "What size beds are there?" The platform will offer up suggestions via a drop-down box with every bed type you can imagine.

Make sure you are extremely accurate in your description. Include details like how many stairs there are up to the property, whether the air-conditioning is just in one room or the whole house and whether there are any spaces that will be shared with others. This is where a lot of hosts come undone and guests will make it known in their review of the property if there are any inaccuracies in your listing.

You can also set house rules for your property and there is a section of the Airbnb listing software that will prompt you to do so. We always suggest a "no-party" policy and if there is a pool, we always write in the house rules that children need to be supervised in the pool and no glass is to be brought into the pool area. These rules will protect you and back up any claims you make if guests cause damage to the property.

STEP 2: Pricing, Fees, and Extras

Pricing your property is one of the most contentious areas of creating an Airbnb listing. Where possible, take advantage of the Airbnb Smart Pricing algorithm where you can enter a minimum and maximum price for your property and Airbnb will determine where the price should sit depending on demand, competitor pricing and events in the area.

> **Where possible, take advantage of the Airbnb Smart Pricing algorithm.**

If you choose to go it alone, I would recommend varying your property's pricing according to demand. If there are events in your local area such as an annual sporting event, show or conference that typically brings in a lot of out-of-town visitors, increase your prices to take advantage of this. You will also want to charge more for weekends and school holiday periods when there will be a greater demand.

Be realistic about pricing. Don't get over-excited and greedy, or you could very well find your occupancy so low that you aren't able to cover your bills. I come across two types of strategies with property owners pricing their homes…

1. A preference for a higher nightly rate and less occupancy if it means less wear-and-tear on their homes.

2. A preference for a higher occupancy and lower nightly rate, for a more regular income. Please note, a lower price doesn't mean a lower quality of guest.

Airbnb will allow you to send special offers or discounts to guests. Initially, when we list a property, we also recommend lowering the nightly rate to a rate too good to pass up to attract initial bookings — and, in turn, reviews. We do this because we know that once we get three or four reviews, the listing will take off and we'll have consistent inquiries.

You need to find the sweet-spot with your pricing and often, if you find your inquiry levels are low, you may be priced too high. You should know your local competition — does your property offer more modern features, is it closer to amenities, do you have a coffee maker? Once you determine your value, you can set an accurate price. We recommend charging a minimum cleaning fee to ensure your time changing sheets is worthwhile.

You can also charge an additional amount per person if you want to set a base price on the property. For example, if your home has a sofa bed and sleeps six people, you may charge a base price of $200 for four people and then $15 per person per night to use the sofa bed. This will cover your time and laundry costs to accommodate the extra people.

So how do pricing and fees work on Airbnb? A typical, one-night booking of a property below shows four guests staying at a property charging $263 per night. There is a cleaning fee of $110 added on and then Airbnb charges a fee of $51 (guest fees are around 19% on top of the nightly rate). So, the total is $424 for the night.

Dates	
07/05/2018 → 07/06/2018	
Guests	
4 guests	˅
$263 x 1 night	$263
Cleaning fee ⓘ	$110
Service fee ⓘ	$51
Total	$424

So, how does that $424 get broken down?

The host will receive…

- Accommodation rate of $263 less 3–5% dependent on cancellation fee = $255.11
- Cleaning Fee = $110

Total = $365.11

Airbnb will receive…

- Service fee charged to guest = $51.00
- Service fee charged to host = $7.89

Total = $58.89

There is a fine line when considering what should be included in an Airbnb stay and added extras that you might charge an additional fee for. Due to the lack of standards in this industry, the review system is the best indicator as to whether a host is crossing boundaries. I recently came across a host who was advertising an "air-conditioned unit" but upon arrival, the guests were told that there was an extra charge for the unit's remotes to operate the air-conditioners.

I have also heard of hosts who charge extra for blankets. Personally, either of these situations would not leave me feeling particularly happy and I highly doubt there would be many guests returning for a second visit once they feel they have been taken advantage of.

So, what *can* you charge an extra amount for and still offer good value for money?

Airport Transfers

Offering an airport pick-up service is one of the most requested added extras from guests, in my experience. There are many hosts who will offer to collect guests for a set rate from the airport to save them the trouble of finding transport. Hosts will need to take into consideration the time they have to put into this service and what will happen should the plane be delayed — will you still be willing to go and collect your guests at midnight?

Extra Time in the Property

Many requests will come in for early check-ins or perhaps a later check-out. If a guest has a flight that leaves late at night, then a 10am check-out might not suit them and they may prefer to stay on in your property until it is time to leave for the Airport. In this case you need to think very clearly about charging extra for the time the guests use your space. Allowing the guest to check out at night may prevent you from taking another booking for that day. Quite a few Hotels have adopted an hourly charge for early check-ins or late check-outs.

Transport

Do you have bikes you could rent out? Perhaps you have another car that you are happy for guests to use? I have seen many hosts offering to hire out their own car or bike in exchange for extra income on Airbnb. Personally, the insurance and liabilities factor scares the hell out of me when I see this — but perhaps you're a risk-taker and want to add this option to your listing?!

Meals

Cooking a meal for guests is another service you could offer in exchange for a fee. I met a host once who rented out her granny flat and would charge a $10 fee for her guests wanting to join her in the main house for dinner. She also offered a breakfast basket with fresh fruit and bread, cereals, and jams delivered to the granny flat in the morning for a $20 fee.

Groceries

Quite a few of your guests will arrive late or might arrive on a public holiday when all the shops are shut. A service guests really appreciate is to offer to go shopping for them so that groceries are in the fridge and pantry when they arrive for their stay. You might decide to charge a small fee for this service on top of the cost of the groceries. It will be much-appreciated and should reflect well in your review.

Baby Furniture Hire

Hosts are known to charge more to arrange a cot or high chair, but personally, I would always recommend a local, professional baby furniture hire company to avoid liability issues. I would hate to think that you have charged a family extra money for a cot only to find that it has collapsed or developed some other kind of fault.

Extra Furniture and Homewares

Often, a request will come through on a booking inquiry asking if we are able to provide extra items in the property. Now, this might be something small such as a salad bowl through to something larger like a barbecue. Our most common request is for an extra bed to accommodate guests' ideal sleeping arrangements.

If we can easily source these items, we charge a fee to cover the transport costs and wear-and-tear of the item. Guests are usually happy to pay and appreciate that we're going above and beyond, which almost always results in a favorable review.

Mid-Stay Cleaning Service

The cleaning fee that guests pay only covers the final exit clean that takes place after they vacate. However, there is an opportunity to upsell a guest to pay for a mid-stay clean or regular servicing of the property if they are staying for a long time in the property. We often have guests that book in for months at a time — a mid-stay clean not only gives us extra income but also an opportunity to inspect the property and ensure guests are looking after it.

Payment for these extra services

I recommend using Airbnb to request and receive payment for extra services and avoid cash transactions. It is important there is a clear record of the transaction for both you and the guest. You can do this easily by clicking the "Request Money" option in the reservation.

Step 3: Availability

The final step to putting together your listing is to set your calendar availability and decide how long you want to host your space for. This is totally up to you — open your calendar up indefinitely or choose to try the concept out for a short time. You can also choose when you want to welcome guests from. Make sure you're truly ready.

You can also set specific boundaries like minimum nightly stays for certain dates or seasons. As a property management company, we choose to always have a one-night minimum as this gives us the

> Open your calendar up indefinitely or choose to try the concept out for a short time.

best chance of being fully booked and filling all gaps in the month. This may not suit all hosts, as it can mean back-to-back bookings and a *lot* of cleaning and laundry!

Set your check-in and check-out times. Don't make the mistake of being too flexible with this option — you need to set boundaries and not become a slave to midnight check-ins. Remember, you can adjust these settings at any time to suit your lifestyle.

Now, your listing is ready to go live!

STEP 4: Handling Enquiries and Guest Communication

As soon as your listing goes live, you need to be prepared to handle guest inquiries and respond to bookings. The easiest and most efficient way to do this is by downloading the Airbnb smartphone app. This way, your phone will notify you as soon as an inquiry comes through. Keep in mind that Airbnb is an international accommodation platform, so you will have inquiries coming through day and night. Once an inquiry comes through about your listing, you can almost guarantee that your potential guest is continuing their search and contacting several other hosts, so you need to respond as soon as possible.

> The easiest and most efficient way to do this is by downloading the Airbnb smartphone app.

There is a very cool feature on the app where you can save set messages and I would recommend that you have a saved message for the initial contact with an enquirer. Perhaps something like…

> "Hi, thank you for making a booking at my property. I look forward to hosting you on your trip and prior to your arrival, I am happy to answer any questions you may have. Please let me know closer to your arrival what time you would like to check in (check-in time is between 2 pm and 8 pm) and I will meet you at the property to give you the keys. Regards, Julie."

Other popular questions you may want to ask are…

- "How many adults and children are in your group?" This is especially important if they only indicate one person on the booking. I have had this happen, only for three more people turn up when I've only prepared the property for one.
- "What brings you to Cairns?" Engaging with the guest may help you to build some rapport with them before they arrive.
- "What bedding configuration suits best? Would you like the sofa bed made up?" I learned the hard way never to assume that a booking for two people means that they are a couple. I once had siblings traveling together but I'd only prepared a queen-sized bed for them. Oh well, we all had a laugh while I made up the sofa bed!

The most important tip I can give you with handling inquiries is to respond quickly to all questions — make sure you read them carefully and respond appropriately. For those of you worried about language barriers, Airbnb has a great translating feature so communication with your International guests is made easy.

As a bonus to readers who want more information on this subject please go to www.milliondollarhost.com.au for -

> *FREE Airbnb Guest Messaging Guide (complete with templates) - as used by Julie George and Host My Home Pty Ltd (valued at $199)

STEP 5: How to Keep Your Listing at the Top of the Airbnb Search List

For anyone familiar with Google algorithms and how hard it is to maintain a 'Page 1' listing, you will be right at home with Airbnb!

> **These algorithms change regularly and there is no way to cheat the system — trust me I've tried!**

These algorithms change regularly and there is no way to cheat the system — trust me I've tried! One of the most common cheats is to put in a different location to take advantage of what tourists would typically search for in your area. Airbnb doesn't allow you to put your location as say, your capital city name instead of your suburb as it works in conjunction with Google Maps and you need to verify the address of any property you list.

So, it comes down to organically climbing your way to the top of the list view. So, how do you do this? Here are a few tips…

- Get more reviews! You want as many (positive ones, that is) as you can get. You'll notice listings that appear on the first page of a search usually have a lot of reviews.

- Turn "Instant Book" on. Guests prefer this, and Airbnb ranks properties in order of what guests are looking for.
- Constantly refresh descriptions, and keep listing content unique and up-to-date.
- Update your photos and change them often. Remember, there are no limits here so add some photos of popular tourist attractions in your area.
- Change your pricing — adjusting your daily price up or down by a dollar is enough.
- Inspire guests to view your listing. Even if they don't end up booking, your listing will rank higher the more clicks it gets. This might be where a unique main photo or listing name will encourage viewers to click through to your listing.
- Avoid declining or canceling bookings. If you reject potential guests, the last thing Airbnb is going to do is reward you with a high ranking.
- Don't be fooled by your browser history. You may think you are ranking highly in your location, but if you clear your history you might see different results.
- As an Airbnb "Superhost", you get a pretty badge and a quicker response from customer services, and you are reassuring future guests about your capabilities, but this won't boost your listing up the ranks.

STEP 6: Congratulations — *Your First Guest is on Their Way!*

A week before a guest is due to arrive, I would suggest that you contact them again to coordinate a check-in time and to find out what transport method the guests will be arriving via so that you can give them directions. Ensure that you give the guest your phone number, address and any other check-in details such as gate codes.

You will also want to conduct an inventory check prior to check-in. I would recommend that before your first guest, you conduct a photo inventory of all surfaces, furniture, appliances and homewares in the property. This will allow for you to check for damages or stolen items after each guest leaves. You will just need to update the inventory if anything changes. Please note, I've not had one item stolen, not even a towel, by any one of the thousands of guests I've hosted at my properties — I love Airbnb guests!

> **Ensure that you give the guest your phone number, address and any other check-in details such as gate codes.**

I would *always* recommend meeting the guest in person. You want to visually identify the guests and gauge whether they are going to look after your property. There are a lot of hosts that prefer to offer self-check-in options for guests such as hiding a key for them or having a coded door lock. This does allow for flexibility, but by meeting the guest in person you have an opportunity to walk them through the property and show them how appliances work, where to find extra blankets and how to lock doors, and reiterate the house rules to them. I found the level of respect also increased and properties are much better looked after if a guest gets to meet the host. If you do offer a self-check-in option, always arrange to drop by the next morning to check on your guest.

It is always a good idea to contact your guests a few days after they check in to ensure they are okay and see if they have any questions.

You don't need to pester them, but it shows you care if you send a quick message. The night prior to check-out, I would recommend you send a message to your guest with details, something like...

> "Just a friendly reminder that check-out tomorrow is at 10 am. Please remove all rubbish from the apartment, turn the air-conditioners off, lock the door and leave the keys in the lockbox. If you leave earlier than 10 am, please let me know so that I can get an earlier start on the cleaning. Have a safe onward journey. Regards, Julie."

STEP 7: The Guest Has Checked Out... Now What?

Below is a checklist that each host needs to go through within a few hours of a property being vacated...

- Are all keys/fobs/remotes accounted for?
- Do a walkthrough of the property and check if anything looks out of place, or is broken/missing. If needed, check against your photo inventory.
- Have the guests left any personal items behind? If so, contact them immediately and arrange to return these items to them. You can arrange for the guest to pay you the postage cost through the Airbnb system (Request Money feature on their reservation).
- Empty any fridge contents or rubbish.
- Strip the beds and remove the linen from the property.
- Test the TV, stereos, etc. to make sure they are all working okay, and no one has stolen the batteries from the remotes — yes, this happens!
- Ensure the air-conditioners, fans, and lights are all turned off before you leave.

- Ensure all windows, doors and garage doors are shut and locked securely.

Reviews/Follow-Up with Guests

Communication with guests after they check out is just as important as it is prior to their arrival. Let them know if anything was left behind, if you were happy or disappointed in the way they left the property, or if there were any damages. This communication should all take place via the Airbnb messaging system, even if you have guests' phone numbers. The reason for this is if there is a situation (perhaps a claim for damages) Airbnb then have evidence of conversations, or of you trying to reach out to guests for an explanation.

> **This communication should all take place via the Airbnb messaging system.**

One tip I would give fellow hosts is to stay in touch with past guests and send a message, perhaps a month or so after they have left your property, to invite them back. Maybe invite their friends or family to return to your property with the incentive of a discount if they return or pass on your details to others. Once again, you want to make sure that messages and return bookings both go through Airbnb. Please don't be tempted to stray from the Airbnb platform to cut out the "middle-man" and its fees. This will mean that you are also straying from the security of the payment collection system, the host guarantee and the support Airbnb offers if something goes wrong.

Guests Caused Damage — Now What?

One of the biggest concerns for property hosts is damage to their property. When I initially listed my first property on Airbnb, one of the first questions I was asked by friends and family was, "What happens if the guest damages your property, or steals something?"

Firstly, the good news is that we have never had any major damage to a property while running our business. Secondly, if there are any damages, guests are usually the first to admit it and offer to pay for repairs. Airbnb's review system holds the power here in that guests would much rather admit they damaged your property and arrange to pay for it than leave it for you to find and then giving them a bad review. It's so different to guests staying in a hotel who will take anything not nailed down. There is no recourse from a hotel stay and the anonymity allows for the worst kind of human behavior to surface.

> "What happens if the guest damages your property, or steals something?"

On the odd occasion, damages have occurred, the problem has been very easy to solve, either with the guest paying for the damages or in the case of guest denial, Airbnb offers a $1 million host guarantee which will cover guest damage in most cases — if you can prove it! You need to ensure you have photos of entire rooms — including close-up, detailed images of any damage — plus quotes or invoices for repairs or replacements for damage or missing items. In some cases, a police report may need to be presented to make a claim against the host guarantee. I would always recommend that you take a full inventory and photos of the property prior to your first guest so that you can track if an item goes missing or there's damage done to the property. Check it thoroughly every time a guest checks out.

The worst-case scenario that I have personally come across was when a group of teenagers booked one of my properties and proceeded to have a wild party. When one of my team went to check the guests out, he found the place trashed. It appeared the guests had urinated on every surface, the linen was wrecked, there was a hole in one of the walls, and the new lounge had been stained and ruined. It was one of the very few times where we wondered if running an Airbnb management company was truly worth it.

After contacting the guests and telling them how disappointed we were with the condition of the home — and what the costs would be for cleaning, repairs, and replacement — we were even more disappointed that they refused to pay or take any responsibility. Needless to say, they got a scathing review from us and I doubt they would have ever been accepted to stay in an Airbnb property ever again.

Another huge issue was that we had to cancel the immediate booking we had in place for guests turning up to this property the day after our party animals had departed. The house was in a terrible state and not fit for anyone to sleep in.

Airbnb was able to assist us in relocating the new guests to another property and assigned a case manager to help us make a claim for damage to the property. We provided detailed photos, plus quotes for plasterers, handymen, steam cleaners, upholsterers and the purchase of new linen and homewares to our case manager.

The process of gathering all the paperwork we needed to submit and having Airbnb evaluate our situation took about four weeks in total, but the good news is that all of our costs were covered, and we were able to get the property back to a functional state.

So, the moral of the story here is that occasionally, you will have damages or bad guests (I can count on one hand the number of bad guests I have seen out of over 3,000 guests that I have had stay at my properties) but as long as you document everything and communicate with Airbnb, you will find the problems will be solved very easily.

Building A Business Using The Airbnb System

Less than 1% of Airbnb hosts have more than two listings — would you like to be in that 1%?

Airbnb has provided the most exciting platform for entrepreneurs, offering several ways to make an income or build a business empire. The most exciting part of this is that you don't even have to own any property to take advantage of these opportunities. You just need to have a business plan and think outside the box.

> **Less than 1% of Airbnb hosts have more than two listings — would you like to be in that 1%?**

Firstly, you need to decide what your goals are and then create a business plan. So, let's start with your goals. Do you want to supplement your current income to save money towards a new car? Are you trying to pay off debts? Do you want to replace your current income and work for yourself? Are you looking for a career change? Or perhaps you are keen to build an empire to create your financial freedom. That last one was my goal and in less than two years, I have achieved it!

If your goal is to be self-employed, that's very different to finding a business model that you can scale up to create a larger company. With self-employment, you may decide that by listing three or four properties yourself (either by leasing/sub-leasing) or by purchasing investment properties, you can run these Airbnb listings by yourself and do all the work involved such as cleaning, without drafting in other people.

On the other hand, if you are fortunate to come across amazing, like-minded, hard-working people that you can employ, you will need to adapt your business structure to scale up and provide employment for others while earning enough income to cover your wage as well. This sounds a *lot* scarier than it is and this is where my own business experience and results may just assist those of you wanting to replicate what I have achieved.

Think outside the box!

Airbnb is a relatively new and exciting concept to a lot of us, offering so many opportunities for third parties to make money off the success of this online platform.

Establish an Airbnb Property Management Company

You can offer to manage Airbnb logistics for other property owners by becoming a Primary Host and creating listings under your profile, so you can offer your services to more clients than you can under the usual restrictions on co-hosting (more about this option later in this chapter). There are three ways to run the property management system in terms of billing.

1. You set listings up to appear under your profile so that guests assume that it is your property they are coming to stay at. You then answer all inquiries, take bookings, arrange to meet guests and care for them during their stay. You may offer to clean the property as well. In the Accounts section of Airbnb, you can set payments up to be split between your account and the owner's, but you can only share a percentage of the total. You can't separate the cleaning fee from the accommodation cost, for instance.

> **There are three ways to run the property management system in terms of billing.**

2. You might have the full amount paid to the owner and then invoice them for your services.

3. The third (and best) option — the one I follow myself, as it happens — is to collect all payments in and then disburse the funds to owners and creditors, before collecting a management fee for your service. If you are collecting income on behalf of a property owner and looking after their property, you will need to get your real estate license and operate a trust account, undergoing regular audits.

So, let's talk about setting up your own property management company! This is exactly what I did in 2016 and it has been an amazing journey. I learned a lot of lessons along the way and trialed many different structures before I finally came to the one I am running now. Reading this book, you'll see that I am not limiting myself to one structure. Rather, I'm flexible, offering services that suit the client's individual needs.

The first step in setting up a similar business to mine is to get a real estate agent license. Now, this will vary in every state and country, but in Queensland, Australia, you need to be a qualified real estate *principal*. You can do this online or in person, and the course is quite detailed, taking you through all aspects of property management, sales and operating trust bank accounts (where property owners' money is held).

Perhaps you already have this license and are exploring ways to offer an alternative to your property owners apart from long-term rentals or sales. There are quite a few existing agents who offer short-term rentals, but very few who have taken advantage of the buzz of Airbnb and mentioned it in their marketing.

When I first started my business, Host My Home Pty Ltd, we weren't reinventing the wheel, but what we were doing was establishing ourselves in the marketplace as Airbnb experts and concentrating on this one target market. The property management side of the business — including running a rent roll with a trust account and having regular Office of Fair Trading audits — is much the same as any local real estate agent would offer.

The point of difference is the "hospitality twist" — taking initial guest inquiries, converting inquiries to bookings, meeting guests on arrival to give them keys and cleaning the property after they depart. If you can imagine combining a real estate agency with a hotel operation, there you have it… an Airbnb property management company!

There are no set standards or operational procedures when it comes to operating an Airbnb property management company. You may decide that your services will not include the cleaning component or that you won't meet guests on-site, but rather have them collect keys at your office. Personally, I'm not a fan of either of these suggestions.

At Host My Home Pty Ltd, we always make a point of meeting our guests face-to-face. If possible, we will welcome them on arrival at the property to give them keys, show them through the home and explain how to use the appliances and lock the door whenever they head out to explore the local area. This meeting gives us the opportunity to welcome guests properly and answer any questions they may have about their stay.

We also get a chance to go over the house rules of the property and ensure the guests are who they described themselves to be online. I want to know that if they have booked for three people, six haven't shown up expecting to stay. I want to know that, although they have promised there will be no parties at the property, they haven't shown up with crates of beer and a drum kit. Once our guests are met and have put a face to the name of the host, the respect level improves dramatically, and we find the property is well looked after as our guests believe they are staying in "Julie's home" — a home that she is extremely proud of.

When it is not possible to meet the guests on arrival in person — for example, if they are arriving at midnight or aren't sure of their arrival time — we will always make a point of dropping by in the morning so that we get that opportunity to meet.

We are very aware that we have been entrusted to care for another person's valued home and take that responsibility very seriously. That is why we have developed key procedures to make sure we check for damages or missing items in the house after a guest vacates. If you are going to set up a property management company yourself, I strongly recommend that this is one of the first procedures you have a plan for. If you aren't looking after a home like it is your own, you will find that the client may take their business elsewhere.

So, when you find a new client, you will need them to sign some paperwork. As well as completing the required property management forms (Form 6, if you're in Queensland), I would also recommend creating a form that asks questions about the home such as…

- "When is bin day?"
- "What are the gate codes?"
- "Are pets allowed?"
- "Where are guests able to park?"

…and anything else that might assist you in not only managing the property but also advising guests. These questions are going to help you write descriptions on the Airbnb listings you will create for your managed properties.

Clearly set out your terms and conditions on a document — there is nothing that kills a business relationship faster than having differing expectations. Get everyone on the same page by clearly writing up a document that includes:

- The fees you charge and when the client can expect to be paid from Airbnb.
- How the client can terminate the agreement.
- What happens to future bookings if the client terminates the agreement. This is important as Airbnb will penalize hosts with monetary fines for canceling — it will also affect your standing with Airbnb.

- How you can terminate the agreement with the client.
- Property insurance information.
- What the owner will need to provide or do to prepare the property for guests and hand it over to you for management.
- What consumables you will be providing for the property and what the clients will need to contribute.
- What will be involved in the "guest clean" — e.g., if you're not going to clean the windows or fans, make it very clear to the property owner so there will be no misunderstandings.
- How you will handle the extra "spring cleaning" that needs doing.
- If you're going to be taking care of any garden and pool maintenance.
- What happens in terms of maintenance, repairs, and replacement of homewares.
- If there are preferred contractors — e.g., electrician or plumber — that the client would like you to use.
- Wi-fi/internet, how it's provided and what happens if the connection fails. This will be one of the first things guests ask for and if the internet connection isn't reliable, you can guarantee this will be the first thing they will complain about.
- Personal use of the property — you need to make it clear to the owner that once you take on the management of the property, they will need to contact you prior to going to the property to ensure there are no guests staying there.

Once your policies and procedures are established, you will find that your business will run smoothly. It took me a long time to establish my policies and procedures, and I often learned the hard way before I wrote them down for new clients to sign off on.

I have had past clients who had a difference of opinion as to what a "guest clean" should entail and were upset that the cushions had not been steam-cleaned in between guests. I also had another client who believed that we should be washing down her pool area every time. This caused quite a bit of friction and we quickly learned to document *everything* in advance so there are no misunderstandings ahead of time.

Once the client is signed up, you will need to arrange to take photos of the property. I would recommend a professional photographer to capture good, marketable images. We often also get floorplans of properties drawn up to be able to show our visitors exactly what to expect during their stay. Once the property has been photographed and you have the signed paperwork back from the owner you can create the listing online.

You need to be extremely accurate, carefully describing what the property offers and what can be found in the local area. When we have rushed a listing in the past, it has failed to get the traction of inquiries and bookings we wanted. Be clever with strategies such as pricing and offer deals in the beginning to encourage your first guests — and first reviews.

As soon as the listing goes live, you need to be prepared for inquiries. Act quickly and accurately when answering these inquiries, to turn them into bookings. You will soon be meeting and greeting your first guests — if you play your cards right. Airbnb allows you to easily manage multiple properties, monitor calendar bookings across your portfolio and keep track of your earnings and progress. It's all very exciting!

You will need to be across all maintenance that needs completion at properties and have a system in place to inform owners or to get the work completed yourself. The cleaning and care of the home including putting the bins out to the kerb on a weekly basis needs to be factored into your workload. Will you do these taks or will you employ someone to help you?

Let me tell you that if you get your business plan right you will very quickly need to consider getting extra assistance to help you grow. This business model is one that I have not only experienced first hand but have seen others adopt and do very well with.

So, what are other ways of making money through the Airbnb system?

Become a Co-Host

Co-hosting on Airbnb is a great option where you do not need a real estate qualification and where your profile is linked to another person's profile and you assist in messaging and managing the inquiries. You might offer your services, including meeting and greeting the guest at the property to show them around and give them keys to the home.

As a co-host, you might also offer to clean the home, do the laundry, and replenish supplies such as toilet paper, milk, coffee, and washing powder.

> As a co-host, you might also offer to clean the home, do the laundry, and replenish supplies .

In the past, there have been limits on how many hosts you can co-host for. This is something to consider when setting up your business plan, which may limit your business expansion.

In August 2018 a change was made to the Co-Hosting function on Airbnb by the way of the removal of the split payment system. Previously the Co-Hosts were able to set a percentage plus the cleaning fee to be paid to them directly by Airbnb. Now you will have to invoice the property owner / primary host for your services and chase up your payments to ensure payments. Another alternative is to set up your bank account details in the Payout feature of the primary hosts listing so that you are paid a portion of the income. **Please note you will not be able to separate the Cleaning Fee in this option.

There are no limits on the services you can offer as a co-host. One way to present yourself as a co-host is to offer a "host relief service", offering to "babysit" a host's property while they take a break. This is a service that we offer at Host My Home and there are two ways of charging for it.

1. You can charge a commission and/or cleaning fee on the bookings you look after.

2. You can charge an hourly rate to co-host the property.

This is a service that we offer and keeps us very busy over the Christmas and New Year period. When we are asked to babysit a property, we conduct a full appraisal of the property to see how long it will take to clean the premises and find out if there is anything additional to be done, such as putting bins out. This helps us provide an accurate quote and work out the best way to charge the property owner.

Leasing/Sub-Leasing

This is the most common business idea thrown around when you hear people talk about making money out of Airbnb without owning property. It is not as easy as it first appears —there are quite a few legal hurdles to jump over and you absolutely must have written permission from the landlord to sub-lease a property on Airbnb.

The first thing I want to clear up is the definition of the term "sub-leasing". You are not, in fact, sub-leasing a property by having guests stay in it. You are not getting those guests to sign a lease, nor can you hold them responsible for paying rent or covering property damage. When you list a rented property on Airbnb, you are responsible for rent, property damage and anything else that you signed the lease to cover.

If you can find a willing landlord who is happy for you to make money out of their property, you can lease the property, create a new listing under your profile and start taking bookings. You are going to have to consider insurance implications and body corporate issues, and you will have to take responsibility for all damages or wear and tear inflicted on the property by your guests. The other major risk with this strategy is that you are responsible for the rent, electricity, wi-fi and any other associated costs, regardless of whether you have any bookings producing income on the property.

> **The first thing I want to clear up is the definition of the term "sub-leasing".**

The hardest part of this business model is to find properties to list on Airbnb. To make this a success, you'll need credibility with property owners and to be highly professional in your approach. I would suggest writing up a professional letter introducing yourself, explaining your business model and your intentions with the property. I would also make an offer too good to refuse, such as a willingness to pay a higher rent, split profits or offer to obtain an extra insurance policy for the contents of the property.

If you have had prior experience in running this business model on other properties, provide evidence or links to Airbnb listings so that the landlord can see reviews from guests on how clean and well-maintained your properties are. Advertising your concept online is another way to gain new clients. Perhaps you can place an online ad, along the lines of...

WANTED

Fully furnished properties in the City suitable to be listed for short-term stays
Above market rents GUARANTEED
Contents and building insurance coverage provided
Call Julie on 2343 4546

You can then interview property owners to see if they are suitable for you. The benefit of this strategy is that you choose the right property that perhaps costs you $300 a week to lease. You can rent it out for $100 a night, so you only need to rent it for four nights to cover rent and other costs. If you rent it for five nights or more, you get to keep all the profit!

List an Experience on Airbnb

One of the newest concepts Airbnb has begun to offer is the "experiences" platform. The concept is currently only offered in a few of Australia's major cities, but it is likely to come to other areas before too long. If you want to develop a business around this opportunity, just imagine the possibilities of being one step ahead of the competition!

Through experiences, hosts can promote day tours or trips that they personally Host in their town. For example, in Melbourne, there are hosts offering shopping experiences, where they take guests shopping for the day, stopping by all the hidden gems that the city has to offer but are often hard to find as a tourist.

> Just imagine the possibilities of being one step ahead of the competition!

One of the most popular is a vintage clothes shopping tour offered by a host who wants to share their passion for vintage clothing with others. For $34 per person, the host will take guests to five of their favorite shops during a two-hour period. A coffee or beverage is provided during the shopping trip. Another popular experience is a pub crawl where for three hours, the host will take guests to four hidden laneway bars. The cost is $49 per person and includes discounted drinks along the way. Can you imagine making a business out of taking people around to bars and drinking every day?

So, why are these experiences so successful? Just as Airbnb offers the opportunity to meet locals and stay in a local residence, tourists who are traveling to your town or city are also looking for a local's perspective when it comes to activities and entertainment. Think back to your past travels and remember what stood out to you about those trips. For me, it is always the people that I meet and the interactions I have with the locals. Sure, the scenery is spectacular, but getting to meet and know the locals has always been the highlight.

So, whether your passion is shopping, drinking, hiking, photography or perhaps kayaking, why not turn your hobby into a business? The best career advice I was ever given was, "Find something you love to do — then find someone to pay you to do it!"

List Your Restaurant/Café/Eatery on Airbnb

Do you run a restaurant or café? One of the newest initiatives Airbnb has put in place is partnering up with local eateries to promote them on their site. In the USA, you can click on the "Restaurants" tab to make a reservation at a local restaurant, notify the owners if you are running late for your booking or pay for your meal in advance. This service is so easy to use that while I was researching it for this book I accidently reserved a table at one of New Yorks Italian restaurants for lunch… oops…. I found it was very easy to cancel reservations as well as make them.

So, if you operate a restaurant in Australia, get ready to list your place now so that you can take full advantage of this feature when it does hit our shores!

Provide Third-Party Services to Hosts

Do you run a gardening business or clean pools for a living? Perhaps you have a cleaning business. The introduction of Airbnb and the thousands of Australian homeowners who have established themselves as mini-hotels means that third-party services now have a huge new target market they can reach out to. Hosting an Airbnb property takes up a *lot* of time. The novelty of cleaning the place every couple of days or keeping the pool clean will soon wear off for a lot of people, and they will look to outsource these jobs.

> **Hosting an Airbnb property takes up a lot of time.**

If you offer a special Airbnb deal for hosts, you could advertise it in a generic way — in newspapers, on social media or radio ads.

Alternatively, you could reach out to property owners and hosts on Airbnb directly, but this is not an easy task. To do so, you need to send an inquiry message, as if you are looking to book that person's property. Make sure you apologize in advance for not wanting to make a booking and explain that you're contacting them to offer a new service in the area. If you can specialize in Airbnb properties, you will have a massive, new market to target.

Once you have a client or two be sure to get testimonials that you can use in your marketing to other similar property owners. You will soon establish yourself as an expert in the Airbnb field this way.

Create a Booking Agency for Airbnb Listings

There are plenty of hosts who are happy to offer a meet-and-greet service and deal with the cleaning of the property but lack the technical ability needed to operate the Airbnb system online or through the smartphone app. What is easy to do for one person is not always easy for others. If you enjoy being attached to your phone night and day and can easily answer inquiries, send messages to guests and update or adjust listings and/or pricing, then you can promote these skills to others.

One of the target markets I have discovered that is very keen for this type of business are existing hotel or holiday apartment managers who have typically used channel managers, computer software programs who work with Booking sites such as Booking.com or Trivago to feed inquiries and bookings to the reservations department of a hotel.

> **What is easy to do for one person is not always easy for others.**

Channel managers in Australia have not yet found a way to include Airbnb in the mix as it is so different from other booking sites. This causes an issue for a busy hotel manager who isn't familiar with Airbnb. Although hotels and motels are not the accommodation type of choice for most Airbnb guests, the beauty of the site is that they are not excluded. There are options when creating a listing to choose the option of a hotel/motel or holiday apartment so that potential guests know exactly what they are getting when they book a stay.

You could create a property listing under the manager's name and profile and then co host yourself to the listing. This way your client will receive positive or negative reviews on their profile as they will be the ones meeting the guests and preparing the property. If you create the profile with a referral from your own profile, you can earn up to $250 in kickbacks from Airbnb for the referral. Keep in mind, you may need to do multiple listings for the motel, depending on how many rooms there are. Once one listing is booked for a certain date, then you will need another listing to encourage more bookings for that time.

You can charge the client for your services via invoice or through the payout system on Airbnb by providing your bank account details with a set percentage when you create the listing.

You will also need to create a communication system with the property owner to keep your calendars synced and prevent double bookings. If you can offer a booking agent service where you can create, monitor and feed inquiries to the motel/hotel, you may just find that you have a great niche business… until someone else in your area reads this book or comes up with the same idea. You could offer this service for experiences and restaurants as well.

Booking Agent Service

11% of Airbnb booking

- Create or update Airbnb listing
- Monitor the messages
- Respond to enquiries
- Update calendars
- Reporting of future bookings

Offer a Consulting Service

Once you gain experience and have an in-depth knowledge of Airbnb, you can sell your knowledge to others. There are a lot of budding hosts that are looking for a mentor to assist them in setting up a property or building their business. At Host My Home Pty Ltd, we have

> There are a lot of budding hosts that are looking for a mentor to assist them in setting up a property or building their business.

used the referral fee from Airbnb to offer a free consultation for new hosts who have never used the Airbnb system before.

At times, Airbnb has paid out $250 for each new host we have set up and created successful listings for. There are conditions attached, such as a minimum spend for the first guest, but this is a brilliant way of meeting new hosts in your area, imparting your knowledge on them and being paid by Airbnb to do it. You get paid once the first guest has stayed with the new host. Consulting can take the form of one-on-one sessions in person or online, seminars — or perhaps you could even write a book!

Earn Travel Credit

> For every one of your friends you can get to sign up to Airbnb, you will be rewarded with travel credit once they have completed their trip.

So, this chapter is about ways to earn income through the Airbnb system, but I figure that a lot of you would like to then spend that money on traveling, so why not look at earning travel credit as well? For every one of your friends you can get to sign up to Airbnb, you will be rewarded with travel credit once they have completed their trip. Many people are now discovering Airbnb, so why not send a link like the one below to your email contact list or place it on Facebook so you can earn some credits for your next holiday?

For those of you who have not yet used Airbnb to travel or set up a Hosting profile, feel free to use my link to do so - www.airbnb.com/c/julieg588

(I love earning my credits and kickbacks from Airbnb!)

Work as a Buyer's Agent with Investors

This business idea is directed to licensed real estate agents. There many budding real estate investors who are looking to jump on the Airbnb bandwagon, but aren't sure what type of property will provide the best return on investment. If you are currently working as a real estate agent in sales and have researched the performance of Airbnb in your area (you can do this with sites such as AirDNA.com, a website providing statistics and data on Airbnb in different locations), you could establish yourself as the "Airbnb expert" in your field, for both buying and selling Airbnb properties in your area.

> There many budding real estate investors who are looking to jump on the Airbnb bandwagon.

SELLING — If you are selling a property, you can do an Airbnb appraisal to determine the potential nightly rate and expected occupancy of a property. Perhaps it has been operated as an existing Airbnb property and has proven returns and future bookings? Keep in mind, banks and lenders in Australia still don't recognize Airbnb/short-term rental income for people applying for loans. They will still want a long-term rental appraisal.

BUYING — Perhaps you can offer your services as a buyer's agent and work in conjunction with other agents in your area? If you can advertise your services to investors, assisting them in identifying, negotiating and purchasing properties that would be ideal for Airbnb, then you may just find your point of difference in a sea of real estate agents.

Where To Find New Listings

One of my major concerns when I started considering Airbnb as a business was where I was going to find new listings and clients. That's also the number-one question others starting their journey into Airbnb property management ask me. There are several different ways you can attract more property owners to entrust their homes to your services.

Traditional Marketing Options

> **Flyers and business cards** — Put together promotional material that displays your services, contact details and special offers to be given out to potential new clients. Remember, you only get one chance to make a first impression, so make sure they're professionally produced and of high quality.
> **Newspaper and magazines** — Please an ad in local print media to inform the public about your business. I would also recommend writing an article for magazines or newspapers to publish. They

> *There are several different ways you can attract more property owners to entrust their homes to your services.*

will often do this in conjunction with an ad sale. This is one of the quickest ways to establish yourself as an Airbnb expert in your local area.
- **Phonebook** — Place an ad in the property management section of your local phonebook. For a reasonably low cost, you can ensure that your contact details are in every household and business in your town.
- **Radio and television** — A more expensive option to spread the word about your new business, but a very effective way to tell your story.

Online Marketing Options

- **Website** — This is an *essential* marketing tool for any business these days. You need a great "shop front" listing your services, prices, testimonials, links to your Airbnb listings, blogs and ways to contact you.
- **Facebook/Instagram/Twitter/etc.** — Social media is the fastest way to get your message to the masses. You don't have to be an expert on it — trust me, I'm not! If you can get your head around one or two platforms and regularly post on these sites, it will pay off. I particularly like Facebook advertising and being able to target a specific audience. For example, I can choose to target 35 to 60-year-olds who have an interest in property investment and real estate. Once I have uploaded an ad or created a post, it will show up on the news feeds of my target market.
- **Google AdWords** — Another way of targeting a specific market online is to pay for an ad campaign to promote your website to people that type in specific words associated with your business.

For example, I might target "Airbnb property management in Queensland" and anyone who searches for this term online will see my website featured at the top of the search list.
- **Gumtree/Craigslist** — There are many websites that now allow you to promote your business for free online. My business placed a very basic ad on Gumtree in the Cairns region and this created a couple of inquiries which turned into listings.

Contacting Existing Hosts

You can do this directly through Airbnb by enquiring about a property in the same way a guest would. I warn you that you will get a mixture of responses when you do this. I tried it myself when I first started my business and out of ten approaches, one owner abuse me for "misusing the Airbnb system" and seven ignored me. However, two agreed that the novelty of managing their own property had worn off and they could use some help.

Networking Opportunities

- **Meet-up groups** — There's a website and app called "MeetUp" that allows you to meet locals who share similar interests to yours. There are quite a few Airbnb host groups that get together and share tips, provide each other with support and socialize. If there isn't one in your local area, why not start one? I did exactly that in Cairns and our first meeting at a local coffee shop saw nine Airbnb hosts come together and get to know each other. My goal with this group was to provide a forum for hosts to help each other out, not an opportunity for me to sell my services. But as relationships blossomed, so did inquiries, and a few hosts that needed a break used Host My Home to cover for them when they went on holiday.

- **BNI** — Business Network International is just one of the networking groups I have belonged to over the years, offering a regular weekly opportunity to address a multitude of business owners who I could promote my services to.
- **Business lunches** — There are plenty of corporate networking events that provide a great venue for you to meet new people and make new contacts that could assist you in your business. Set yourself a goal to go to one networking event a week when you first start up, introduce yourself and hand out business cards. Follow up this initial meeting with a phone call or email to arrange a one-on-one meeting.
- **Tell everyone what you're doing...** you just never know when casual conversations will turn into a new client. Just this week, I answered a phone call at 9 pm from a very irate homeowner. "There are guests staying at your property who are making too much noise — this is the second night in a row!" Asking the address of the property, it turned out it was not one of the places I manage. However, rather than hanging up on this man, I proceeded to offer advice, helped him find the contact details for the host and even offered to contact them for him. He called me back only minutes later to say he was so impressed with the way I handled the situation that he would like to give me two referrals for properties he would like managed. You just never know when opportunity will come knocking!

Professional Referrals

Most of my referrals come from real estate agents in my local area. I have established my business to complement — not compete — with local agents, and you can do this too. Agents are often looking for an alternative option for property investors, and if you can provide a solution to their problem, you'll find they will be your biggest supporters. So, what can you do to get agents on board?

Provide sales tools for them by way of Airbnb appraisals on properties they are trying to sell. Using AirDNA and other research tools online, it is very easy to come up with an estimate on the price a property would be listed at on Airbnb. Our appraisals always factor in comparable properties in the area. We take into consideration the location and size of the property, how many it can sleep, how many bathrooms it has, what amenities it offers and the demand it might see on Airbnb at different times of the year.

> **I have established my business to complement — not compete — with local agents.**

You must be very careful to not make any guarantees or promises with these appraisals, or it can come back to bite you. Real estate agents might then be able to provide these estimates to potential property investors and as the numbers will be higher than long-term rental income, it could seal the deal with investors wanting a good return. Unfortunately, property valuations in Australia don't recognize short-term rental income as reliable, but a savvy investor will see the potential and it might just get a sale completed for an agent.

Of course, the next question a property investor might pose to an agent is, "How could I logistically run this Airbnb property?" That is where your services come in, and you may very well end up managing the property. It's a win-win! If there's an agent in your area who is supporting your business, you can feed them sales referrals in return. Your clients may find they need to sell in the future and they will trust your opinion.

Another way to work with the agents is to bring them buyers. I've had quite a few property owners wanting to replicate the success of the first property they listed with me that they will ask me to source another one for them. There is nothing that builds a relationship with a real estate agent faster than setting up a buyer to purchase their property.

Finder's Fee

Tell all your family and friends that you are looking for new clients. Offer up a $100 finder's fee and watch your new "sales team" leap into action. You could promote this offer on social media and quickly spread the word that there is a new service in your local area and you are paying a finder's fee for referrals that turn into clients.

My Secrets To Success

Surround Yourself with a Great Team

You can't grow an empire on your own. Although I am the face of Host My Home Pty Ltd, it takes a lot of people to make it successful. You need to find like-minded, trustworthy people that you can delegate to and feel supported by. One of the questions I get asked is how to "scale up". This is one of the biggest challenges I faced for a couple of reasons...

- Who could I trust?
- Was I going to provide enough work for them to survive on?
- How was I going to afford staff?

Find good people that are more skilled than you at certain tasks. There are going to be skills you possess and tasks you enjoy more than others and you need to find a team that compliments that.

> You can't grow an empire on your own.

Trust is a huge challenge for me. I was allowing my team to represent me in the field. My name and photo are on my profile, yet often, it would be one of my co-hosts that would meet guests. I had to feel confident that these people were going to be as welcoming as I would be, treat guests with the respect I would and be prepared to be as patient as me with our non-English-speaking guests.

I have been lucky that everyone in my team has stepped up to show guests the very best example of hospitality, resulting in thousands of five-star reviews on Airbnb. I am so proud when I read how guests enjoyed being personally welcomed at the property and appreciated the time and effort shown by my co-host. I do giggle when "Julie" receives a glowing review, but it was actually one of my male co-hosts!

Recruiting the right people to work with me was always a challenge. Whenever I have advertised and interviewed applicants for positions, I tend to go more on gut feeling and instinct than what is written on their CV. My problem is that I want to see the best in everyone, so I always have a second person interview with me to stop me from creating jobs for the ten people we just saw. However, once you find the right person for your business, I would recommend doing whatever you can to keep them.

I like the idea of giving my team ownership of their duties (I want them to be proud of their achievements), flexibility in their work conditions (I want them to have a life) and be remunerated above the average pay conditions of the industry.

Take a Risk — What's the Worst That Could Happen?

You only have one life, so why not make the most of it? If you have a business idea, give it a try. Yes, it will take up a lot of your time. Yes, it will cost you money. Yes, it might not be successful. But at least you will have given it a go and maybe, just maybe, you could make that business idea a huge success!

The lifestyle you are currently living will not be improved without hard work and determination. I have heard some brilliant business ideas suggested by my family and friends that often never see the light of day — I think that's a shame.

> You only have one life, so why not make the most of it?

The most successful business ideas I've seen throughout my life are those created by super-confident people who believe in themselves. They ignore the naysayers and challenges in their way and just make it happen. There's no reason we can't all adopt this attitude and be courageous enough to give it a go... what's the worst that could happen?

Dream Big and Scale

Every goal starts with a dream, so start dreaming and don't limit yourself by believing you aren't in a position to make these dreams a reality!

Remember, my Airbnb journey only commenced in 2016 and now, in 2018, I'm writing a book, sharing ideas on how to make millions through the sharing economy platform. So, you see, it doesn't take long to change your life for the better.

> Every goal starts with a dream.

Once you have dreamt of the life you would like to live, set yourself goals on how to achieve it. Write your goals down and break them down into smaller steps so that you aren't overwhelmed. Take one step at a time and make every day count towards your vision.

If any of the business ideas in this book have appealed to you, then your next step when you've finished reading is to set a course of action. Ask yourself...

- What goals do I want to achieve?
- How will I break down the steps to achieve these goals?
- What will I do today to take my first step?

And then, as Nike says... just do it!

Our Office in Cairns QLD

Once you have achieved your goals, I would love to hear about your success, so please email me at julie@milliondollarhost.com.au and tell me all about it!

If you need further help in achieving your goals and would like to undertake more training, consult with my team or discuss our mentoring program (where we will replicate our business model in your home town), please go to www.milliondollarhost.com.au.

If you would like to learn more about Host My Home Pty Ltd please go to www.hostmyhome.com.au

If you have enjoyed reading Million Dollar Host and would like more information from Julie George please go to

www.milliondollarhost.com.au

JULIE IS GIVING READERS

*FREE Airbnb Guest Messaging Guide (complete with templates) – *as used by Julie George and Host My Home Pty Ltd*

(valued at $199)

www.ingramcontent.com/pod-product-compliance
Lightning Source LLC
Chambersburg PA
CBHW071353080526
44587CB00017B/3089